Keeping Open the Doo
The Legacy of Vati

Bishop Donal Murray lectured in Moral Theology in Mater Dei Institute and in Holy Cross College from 1969 to 1982. He was Auxiliary Bishop of Dublin from 1982 to 1996 and then Bishop of Limerick until 2009. He is now retired.

Keeping Open the Door of Faith

THE LEGACY OF VATICAN II

BISHOP DONAL MURRAY

VERITAS

Published 2012 by Veritas
7–8 Lower Abbey Street
Dublin 1, Ireland
publications@veritas.ie
www.veritas.ie

ISBN 978-1-84730-369-1

10 9 8 7 6 5 4 3 2 1

All Scripture quotes, except where indicated as being taken from the *New American Bible* (NAB), revised edition, United States Conference of Catholic Bishops, 2011, are taken from the *New Revised Standard Version* Bible, copyright © 1989 National Council of the Churches of Christ in the United States of America. Used by permission. All rights reserved. All quotes from Vatican II documents are taken from *The Basic Sixteen Documents, Vatican Council II*, Fr Austin Flannery OP (general editor), New York/Dublin: Costello Publishing/Dominican Publications, 1996.

Cover image photo by Hank Walter/Time & Life Pictures/Getty Images.

A catalogue record for this book is available from the British Library.

Designed by Lir Mac Cárthaigh, Veritas

Printed in Ireland by Turners Printing Limited, Longford

Veritas books are printed on paper made from the wood pulp of managed forests. For every tree felled, at least one tree is planted, thereby renewing natural resources.

Contents

INTRODUCTION

AS THE YEAR 2000 approached, Blessed John Paul II, who had himself participated in the Second Vatican Council, referred to Vatican II as 'this great gift of the Spirit to the Church at the end of the second millennium'.[1] Looking towards the coming millennium he asked to what extent the fruits of the Council could be seen in the Church. This year, 2012, fifty years after the Council opened, is a good opportunity to reflect again on that question.

A complete examination of all the rich teaching of the Council and how it has been implemented is clearly beyond the scope of this book – or perhaps of any book. What is written here is one person's reflections on five themes of the Council and their implications for today's world.

The first is the concept of *communion*. The special Synod of Bishops convened on the twentieth anniversary of the conclusion of Vatican II identified this as the central idea of the Council. It is more important than ever. It is also the theme of the International Eucharistic Congress in Dublin in the year of the fiftieth anniversary of the opening of the Council.

One of the greatest challenges for the Church is to overcome the perception that it is primarily an institution, out of touch, insensitive, concerned only with defending its position. The Church is called to be something quite different – a communion with God and with one another. Structures are necessary but they have no other purpose than to facilitate growth in union with God and with one another. The purpose of the Church is to be 'a sign and instrument … of communion with God and of the unity of the entire human race.'[2] Living up to that purpose is a priority for all of us in a world where institutions are distrusted, a world marked by alienation rather than communion.

---

1. JOHN PAUL II, *Tertio Millennio Adveniente*, 36.
2. VATICAN II, *Lumen Gentium*, 1.

The second priority is the idea of *mission*. Vatican II issued an urgent call to all Christians to recognise that the entire Church and every member of the Church has a part to play in bringing the Good News to a world which needs to hear the words of hope and the call to share in God's life, which are the fundamental truths of human life. That call should never be thought of as intended only for particular groups and individuals. Each parish and each individual within it is meant to be a missionary. The great missionary tradition of Ireland, which has shaped the Church in many parts of the world, was not just the tradition of those who went to distant places, but also of the families, villages and towns in which they learned the faith they carried to the ends of the earth.

That points to a third theme, the importance given by the Council to the role of every member of the Body of Christ in the life of the Church, and in particular *the role of the lay faithful*. Soon after the Council ended, I wrote an article in a student magazine in Maynooth which said:

> This more active Christianity will involve a growing sense of responsibility for the Church and this in turn will lead to the increasingly vocal laity which will perhaps be the most striking development in the Church's life in the next half century.[3]

The role of the laity, the priesthood, of all believers and the responsibility of every Christian for the Church are truths reemphasised by the Council. Although much has changed for the better in the intervening years, a fuller understanding and implementation of these concepts are urgently necessary.

---

3. MURRAY, D., 'The New Theology and the Christian Life', *Maynooth* (formerly *The Silhouette*), 1966, p. 42.

The fourth theme is the central place given by the Council, and by the Popes who followed it, to the understanding of *the human person* in the light of the Gospel. This is of particular importance in our day, when the rights of the individual are rightly emphasised – if not always respected[4] – but where a rich understanding of the meaning of human dignity and of the destiny of human life is sadly lacking. Here is a starting point, identified by Pope Benedict on the day of the inauguration of his ministry as Pope. Speaking of the many deserts in the world – poverty, loneliness and so on – he said:

> There is the desert of God's darkness, the emptiness of souls no longer aware of their dignity or the goal of human life. The external deserts in the world are growing, because the internal deserts have become so vast.[5]

Finally, there is the theme which is fundamental to all the rest – the question of *faith*, the difficulty and the crucial importance of belief in the world of the third millennium. There is no more fundamental question about us and about our world than the question of God and of how we relate to our Creator and Redeemer. Many people, including believers, live most of their lives in practice as though God did not exist, as though God had 'disappeared from their existential horizon'.[6] That profoundly affects how we see ourselves, how we understand our freedom, how we look on our society.

The door of faith opens up a new vision of ourselves and of our world because it ushers us 'into the life of communion with God'.[7]

---

4. See JOHN PAUL II, *Evangelium Vitae*, 18.
5. BENEDICT XVI, Homily at the Mass for the beginning of his Petrine Ministry, 24 April 2005.
6. JOHN PAUL II, to the Secretariat for Non-Believers, 5 March 1988.
7. BENEDICT XVI, *Porta Fidei*, Apostolic Letter, announcing the Year of Faith, 1.

Vatican II was about renewing commitment to the Gospel proclaimed by Christ and entrusted to the Apostles and to the whole Church to be lived and shared. Pope Paul VI referred to that heritage when he opened a Year of Faith only a couple of years after the Council:

> The Ecumenical Council, just celebrated, recalled these things (cf. *Dei Verbum*, 7), and urged us to go back to these sources of the Church's and to see in the faith the Church's constitutive principle, the first condition of the Church's growth, the basis of its inner security and strength of its vitality in the world.[8]

There are other themes that could have been chosen, for instance the renewal of the liturgy which was the earliest and most obvious fruit of the Council. I have only touched on that and on the question of the place of Scripture in the Church, the issue of ecumenism and many other highly significant aspects of Vatican II. My hope is that this book may play some part in encouraging readers, as individuals and as groups, to take up the documents of the Council and to find nourishment in them for their lives and their communities. I hope that it may help people to respond to the invitation given to Timothy by Paul to 'pursue faith' (2 Tm 2:22):

> We hear this invitation directed to each of us, that none of us grow lazy in the faith. [Faith] is the lifelong companion that makes it possible to perceive, ever anew, the marvels that God works for us. Intent on gathering the signs of the times in the present of history, faith commits every one of us to become a living sign of the presence of the Risen Lord in the world. What the world is in particular need of today is the

---

8. PAUL VI, Homily at the Inauguration of the Year of Faith, 29 June 1968.

credible witness of people enlightened in mind and heart by the word of the Lord, and capable of opening the hearts and minds of many to the desire for God and for true life, life without end.[9]

✠DONAL MURRAY

February 2012

---

9. *Porta Fidei*, 15.

CHAPTER ONE

The Central and Fundamental Idea

ON 25 JANUARY 1959, in the Basilica of St Paul, Pope John XXIII indicated his intention to convoke the Second Vatican Council. In 1985, at the same place on the same date, Pope John Paul II announced that he was summoning a special meeting of the Synod of Bishops to mark the twentieth anniversary of the closing of the Council. The purpose of the special Synod would be to 'reflect on, deepen and promote the application of the teachings of Vatican II'.[1] The final Report of that Synod was clear about the key to achieving that goal:

> The ecclesiology of communion is the central and fundamental idea of the Council's documents.[2]

There were those who saw the Synod's report as rowing back from the emphasis of the Council on the idea of the Church as the People of God – a phrase not often used in the Synod's final report.[3] This concern underestimated the richness of the concept of communion. Every bit as much as the image of the Church as 'People of God', the concept of communion expresses the truth that all members of the Church are one in Christ and therefore one with each other through Baptism:

---

1.   JOHN PAUL II, Address at the conclusion of the Extraordinary Synod, 7 December 1985 (my translation).
2.   *The Final Report of the Extraordinary Synod*, b.C.1.
3.   See PANICCIA, P., *1985 Extraordinary Synod 25 Years On*, http://vatican2voice. org/7reception/extra_synod.htm; accessed 6 March 2012.

Fundamentally it is a matter of communion with God through Jesus Christ, in the Holy Spirit. This communion is had in the Word of God and in the sacraments. Baptism is the door and the foundation of communion in the Church. The Eucharist is the source and the culmination of the whole Christian life. The communion of the eucharistic Body of Christ signifies and produces, that is, builds up, the intimate communion of all the faithful in the Body of Christ which is the Church (1 Cor 10:16).[4]

The fundamental importance of 'the intimate communion of all' is crucial to a deepening and promoting of the lessons of Vatican II. The challenge is more urgent than ever. This is a world in which many people feel a strong sense of alienation and disaffection towards Church and State and institutions of every kind.

The economic collapse and the irresponsibility that led to it heightened something that was already endemic in contemporary culture. Life has become more anonymous and more individualistic. People feel swamped by events over which they have no control. The financial crisis is the latest such event. Citizens increasingly feel that they have no voice in society.

Civil unrest in many areas of the world, from the 'Arab Spring' to the London riots, in spite of very different contexts, is often accompanied by expressions of distrust of institutions and governments. Even in countries without turbulent protests, one hears complaints that 'nobody is listening to ordinary people'. If we do not recognise that wider context, we risk misinterpreting what is at stake in individual instances of disaffection. But let us begin with the Church, which is the main concern of this reflection.

---

4. *The Final Report*, b.C.1.

THE 'INSTITUTIONAL CHURCH'

One sometimes hears complaints about the Church which are followed by the statement that 'our parish is fine' or 'our priest is wonderful'. By contrast, the Church at diocesan and universal level – which seems to be the main location of what is called 'the institutional Church' – often appears to provide little sense of belonging or participation. Life has become more complicated and more globalised, and Church life is no exception; the flow of communication, rather than increasing participation, can lead to a feeling of being overwhelmed.

The more complex and distant an institution appears to be, the greater the risk of alienation. Indeed, the term 'the institutional Church' is rarely used except by people who wish to see themselves as dissociated from it. That is not surprising. If one thinks of the Church primarily as an institution, its profound meaning as a mystery, as a sacrament of God's presence and action, as the Body of Christ is lost. In particular what is lost is an understanding of the Church as communion with God and with one another – the Church as a community to which one belongs.

Anything that is seen primarily as an institution, as a structure, cannot but be alienating. Institutions by definition do not empathise. An institution is a structure in which people work in the pursuit of common goals. People working within the institution may be understanding and generous, but the institution *as such* is only a structure which is, or ought to be, at the service of people.

Attempting to deal with the sense of being disaffected by reasoned arguments will never resolve people's sense of alienation. This was startlingly illustrated by the enthusiastic reaction in July 2011 to Taoiseach Enda Kenny's speech attacking 'the Vatican'. In the course of that speech he entirely misrepresented a statement issued by the then Cardinal Ratzinger.[5] The speech rightly reflected people's disgust at child abuse and the devastation of young lives. But it also all too accurately reflected an atmosphere which would tolerate exaggeration and distortion but which would not countenance any voice which might point to other dimensions of the issue. Thus the speech opened with a very specific allegation which, astonishingly, did not seem to refer to anything in particular.

The Holy See's response was dismissed as legalistic because it carefully addressed the explicit charges made by the Taoiseach. The fact that the response pointed out the inaccuracy of statements in the speech was seen as beside the point. An exchange that took place in a pub soon after the speech colourfully illustrates this attitude. One drinker was enthusing about Mr Kenny's words. When a companion objected that a great deal of what he said was simply not true, the response, which has to be toned down somewhat for publication, was 'Who cares about that!'

'THE WHOLE COMMUNITY OF BELIEVERS'

The phrase 'institutional Church' evokes a picture reminiscent of the valley of dry bones described by Ezekiel (37). It is the picture that emerges when one views the Church without any reference to the spirit which gives it life. Every community or human activity appears as a mere structure or a pointless exercise to someone who does not understand why and how people are involved in it. Someone who has no interest in football expresses puzzlement about how so much excitement can be generated by people kicking a ball around a field. There can be no realistic contribution to 'deepening and promoting' the insights of Vatican II without a serious effort to understand the nature of the Church and its life.

---

5. An Taoiseach, Enda Kenny, T.D., Dáil Éireann, 20 July 2011. The document referred to was the Congregation for the Doctrine of the Faith's Instruction *Donum Veritatis, On the Ecclesial Vocation of the Theologian* (1990).

We rightly wish for a renewal of the community of Christ's followers. It must first be a renewal open to the Spirit who gives life. The bringing of new life to the valley of dry bones is a powerful image: 'Thus says the Lord God: From the four winds come, O spirit, and breathe into these slain that they may come to life. I prophesied as he told me, and the spirit came into them; they came alive and stood upright, a vast army' (Ez 37:9, 10).

If renewal is to be real, it needs a growing recognition of who we are at every level in the Church: we are God's family, God's People, the Body of Christ. Structural issues are neither the starting point nor the key to renewal. Structures need to be strengthened, but never for their own sake. The structures of the Church exist for the sake of the communion of all the baptised in their response to Christ, not vice versa:

> This is *of fundamental importance for understanding the Church in her own essence,* so as to avoid applying to the Church – even in her dimension as an 'institution' made up of human beings and forming part of history – criteria of understanding and judgement which do not pertain to her nature. Although the Church possesses a 'hierarchical' structure, nevertheless this structure is totally ordered to the holiness of Christ's members.[6]

In addressing the Roman Curia a few months earlier, the Pope had made the same point even more clearly:

> Mary, the Immaculate One, precedes all others, including, obviously, Peter and the apostles, not only because Peter and the apostles, belonging to the great mass of the human race who, born under the weight of sin, form part of the Church 'holy (yet) made up of sinners', but also because their triple

---

6. JOHN PAUL II, *Mulieris Dignitatem,* 27 (italics in original).

function [teaching, sanctifying and leading] *has no other aim* than to form the Church according to that ideal of sanctity which is already planned and prefigured in Mary.[7]

The Church is first of all to be understood as a 'we', not as an institution or a structure. It is the communion of those who have heard, and seek to accept and to live by, the Word of God revealed in Christ. In the community of faith, we hear and respond to God's invitation into 'the intimate communion of all'. The 'door and foundation' of that communion is Baptism,[8] the sacrament through which we form one body in Christ.

The 'we' is bigger than any one of us, or any group of us. The real meaning of participation can be distorted and diminished by failing to understand that we respond to a word that has been spoken to all humanity in every time and place. The truth of faith is too large to be confined to our situation or to be viewed as the answer only to our expectations:

> When we say: 'We are Church' – well, it is true: that is what we are, we are not just anybody. But the 'we' is more extensive than the group that asserts those words. The 'we' is the whole community of believers, today and in all times and places. And so I always say: within the community of believers, yes, there is as it were the voice of the valid majority, but there can never be a majority against the apostles or against the saints: that would be a false majority. We are Church: let us be Church, let us be Church precisely by opening ourselves and stepping outside ourselves and being Church with others.[9]

7.   JOHN PAUL II, Address to the Roman Curia, 22 December 1987, quoted in *Mulieris Dignitatem*, 27n (my italics).
8.   *The Final Report*, b.C.1.
9.   BENEDICT XVI, Address in the Seminary Chapel, Freiburg im Breisgau, 24 September 2011.

COMMUNION WITH GOD

It is little wonder that the concept of communion with God is not well understood in a world that leaves little room for silence and reflection. Life today is full of activity, stimuli and priorities. The human mind has in many ways 'wilted under the weight of so much knowledge and little by little has lost the capacity to lift its gaze to the heights'.[10] It is not easy to respond to the God who is not just one among the many claims on our attention but who is to be loved with *all* our heart and soul and strength.[11]

Even in a quieter, simpler world, the truth about ultimate reality could never be fully grasped. God is infinitely greater than our minds. Saint Augustine said, 'If you comprehend him, it is not God you comprehend.'[12] What we can learn about God always falls short of the reality; nevertheless to reach some knowledge of God is the most valuable of all truths.[13] Christ, by revealing the mystery of his Father, reveals to us the deepest truth about ourselves, our world and our destiny.[14]

That truth is in harmony with what is deepest in our nature; it is the truth about the destiny for which we were created; it can find an echo in every human heart. We are called to live in communion with God and with one another in Christ, and to live eternally in the fullness of that communion. That is not just a truth about us; it is the truth of who we are.

The Second Vatican Council summed up the intention of its document on the Church in these words:

> Since the Church is in Christ like a sacrament or as a sign and instrument both of a very closely knit union with God and of the unity of the whole human race, [the Council]

---

10. JOHN PAUL II, *Fides et Ratio*, 5.
11. Cf. Deut 6:5, Mk 12:30 and parallels.
12. AUGUSTINE, Sermon 117, 5.
13. Cf. AQUINAS, *Summa Theologiae*, 1, q 12, a 7.
14. Cf. *Gaudium et Spes*, 22.

desires now to unfold more fully to the faithful of the Church and to the whole world its own inner nature and universal mission.[15]

It would be naive to think that an awareness of the inner nature and mission of the Church can simply be assumed as obvious without any reflection or effort. The whole of the Christian life is founded on 'the encounter with an event, a person, which gives life a new horizon and a decisive direction'.[16] Any friendship which changes the direction of one's life requires commitment, thought, generosity and readiness to learn. Friendship with God's only Son, who reveals to us the faithful, merciful, unlimited love of the Father, requires readiness to be changed and a willingness to listen which will affect every aspect of ourselves.

FOUNDED ON PRAYER
The life of the Church, which is communion with God in Christ, has to be founded on prayer. Any renewal that does not begin from there is doomed to be shallow and transitory:

> There is a temptation which perennially besets every spiritual journey and pastoral work: that of thinking that the results depend on our ability to act and to plan. God of course asks us really to cooperate with his grace, and therefore invites us to invest all our resources of intelligence and energy in serving the cause of the Kingdom. But it is fatal to forget that 'without Christ we can do nothing' (cf. Jn 15:5).

> It is prayer which roots us in this truth. It constantly reminds us of the primacy of Christ and, in union with him, the primacy of the interior life and of holiness. When this

---

15. *Lumen Gentium,* Dogmatic Constitution on the Church, 1.
16. BENEDICT XVI, *Deus Caritas Est,* 1.

principle is not respected, is it any wonder that pastoral plans come to nothing and leave us with a disheartening sense of frustration?[17]

If our pastoral plans seem to come to nothing, this may mean that our efforts are not sufficiently rooted in prayer. Have we busied ourselves with making everything work more efficiently according to *our* plans without taking time to reflect on the overriding consideration that the only purpose of our exertions is to cooperate with what God is doing?

Pope John Paul did not mince his words:

> Let us have no illusions: unless we follow this spiritual path, external structures of communion will serve very little purpose. They would become mechanisms without a soul, 'masks' of communion rather than its means of expression and growth.[18]

The tyranny of efficiency makes us uneasy about 'wasting time'. There is an urge to 'get down to business'. This is particularly harmful in Church bodies and in parish life. While we must work as effectively as we can, the work we are doing is not ultimately our own. The warning of Pope John Paul to priests and religious in Maynooth is always relevant. Work for the Lord will not bear fruit if we neglect the Lord of the work:

> We must find time, we must make time, to be with the Lord in prayer ... It is only if we spend time with the Lord that our sending out to others will be also a bringing of him to others.[19]

17. JOHN PAUL II, *Novo Millennio Ineunte*, 38.
18. Ibid., 43.
19. JOHN PAUL II, Address to Priests, Missionaries and Religious, Maynooth, 1 October 1979.

No parish meeting, no planning of a church activity should take place without prayer. Such prayer should leave room for some reflection about the nature of the work that we undertake. Without an atmosphere of prayer there is a danger of acting as if our efforts alone could bear the fruit. There is also a danger that we will finish up doing the wrong work. It is not just a matter of providing efficient machinery and well-run organisations, important though that is. It is a matter of genuinely absorbing a conviction about the purpose of all that we do. Like every structure in the Church, groups and organisations 'have no other aim' but to strengthen and deepen our acceptance of the gift that God offers. If that conviction is not constantly recalled and reflected on, efforts at developing the life of the parish and of the people of the parish will be on the wrong track.

THE GREAT CHALLENGE FACING US

Communion with the Father in Christ must involve communion with each other in Christ. It would be difficult to overstate the importance of this in the context of a moment in history where there is such a strong current of disillusionment with institutions and such a sense for many people that they do not count. The concept of the Church as a communion is essential not only for the well-being of the Church but also for society.

Alienation and disaffection are problems for the whole of society. Communion is in complete contrast to alienation; alienation is the absence of communion. Christ, our Peace, has made divided groups one and has broken down walls of hostility.[20]

Disaffection in society is the product of the loss of a shared vision which can give a sense of common purpose. Communion with God and with one another is the ultimate realisation of such a shared vision. The witness of a vibrant life of communion could offer an antidote to alienation in every area.

---

20. Cf. Eph 2:14.

At the beginning of the new millennium Blessed John Paul wrote about the importance of making the Church a place where communion is 'at home', a place in which communion is learnt:

> To make the Church the home and the school of communion is the great challenge facing us in the millennium which is now beginning, if we wish to be faithful to God's plan and respond to the world's deepest yearnings.[21]

The first decade of the new millennium is already over.

In a world of information overload, it is easy to be swamped by peripheral issues and to miss what is essential. The richness of the documents produced by Vatican II and by recent Popes can make it difficult, even for those who carefully study these writings, to prioritise among all that wealth of material. It has been rightly said that it will take many decades to digest the work of Pope John Paul. In this instance, however, by speaking of 'the great challenge facing us in the millennium which is now beginning', he left his readers in no doubt about the importance of what he was saying.

Has that clear message had the resonance that he intended it to have? How far is the community of faith, in Ireland or elsewhere, even aware that the Pope identified this as 'the great challenge'? Has it in any consistent way been seen as a priority? Here is an unmistakeable indication of the need to reflect on the message of Vatican II. 'The central and fundamental idea' of the Council and 'the great challenge' of Blessed John Paul are still not central to our thinking.

The greatest pastoral challenge of today lies in the fact that so many people see the Church not primarily as a communion but as an institution. This is a huge obstacle to real participation and belonging to the life and mission of the Church. It distorts many

---

21. *Novo Millennio Ineunte*, 43.

aspects of Church life by allowing them to be seen first of all as 'issues' rather than as matters to be reflected on in communion with God and one another. It obscures the power of the Gospel to expand and enrich human horizons.

Furthermore, it seriously diminishes the contribution that the Church can make to the world which is losing a sense of vision and is prey to disillusionment. It is more important than ever that we should be seen as the home and school and sign of 'communion with God and the unity of the whole human race'.[22]

PARTICULAR CHALLENGES OF BUILDING COMMUNION

It is in the community of believers that each of us can learn: 'We can only ever believe within the "we".'[23] It is the responsibility of each believer to reflect and to learn by 'opening ourselves and stepping outside ourselves' and by growing in understanding of the gift of truth entrusted to the 'we' of the Church in every time and culture:

> On the one hand the Gospel message cannot be purely and simply isolated from the culture in which it was first inserted (the biblical world or, more concretely, the cultural milieu in which Jesus of Nazareth lived), nor, without serious loss, from the cultures in which it has already been expressed down the centuries; it does not spring spontaneously from any cultural soil; it has always been transmitted by means of an apostolic dialogue which inevitably becomes part of a certain dialogue of cultures.[24]

'The great challenge' is to engage in dialogue with contemporary culture in a way which allows the community of Christ's followers to be seen for what it is – the sign and instrument by which

---

22. *Lumen Gentium*, 1.
23. Address in the Seminary Chapel, 24 September 2011.
24. JOHN PAUL II, *Catechesi Tradendae*, On Catechesis in our Time, 53.

God builds communion. Pope John Paul identified some of the elements that this would require. Having said that without a spirituality of communion Church structures would be soulless, he went on:

> Consequently, the new century will have to see us more than ever intent on valuing and developing the forums and structures which, in accordance with the Second Vatican Council's major directives, serve to ensure and safeguard communion.[25]

He indicated that the Petrine ministry of the Pope and the working of episcopal collegiality 'need to be examined constantly in order to ensure that they follow their genuinely evangelical inspiration'. He added that 'there is certainly much more to be done in order to realise the potential' of the Roman Curia, Synods of Bishops and Episcopal Conferences as instruments of communion 'in view of the need to respond promptly and effectively to the issues that the Church must face in these rapidly changing times'.[26]

Speaking of the Church at more local levels, he said:

> There, relations between Bishops, priests and deacons, between Pastors and the entire People of God, between clergy and Religious, between associations and ecclesial movements must all be clearly characterised by communion.[27]

He points to the importance of councils of priests and pastoral councils and goes on:

> To this end, we need to make our own the ancient pastoral wisdom which, without prejudice to their authority,

---

25. *Novo Millennio Ineunte*, 43.
26. Ibid., 44.
27. Ibid., 45.

encouraged Pastors to listen more widely to the entire People of God. Significant is Saint Benedict's reminder to the Abbot of a monastery, inviting him to consult even the youngest members of the community: 'By the Lord's inspiration, it is often a younger person who knows what is best.' And Saint Paulinus of Nola urges: 'Let us listen to what all the faithful say, because in every one of them the Spirit of God breathes.'[28]

These passages show that a renewal focussed on building communion demands far more than an adjustment of structures. It will mean giving practical effect to the principle that the structures of the Church have no other aim than to foster holiness. Holiness and communion are closely linked; holiness consists in the unity with and in Christ which finds its expression in communion.

We need to find ways of understanding one another and listening to one another. But we can only do so if we learn to listen to Christ. The very nature of communion with him – reaching across every time and place – means that questions of a doctrinal nature cannot be decided by individual parts of the Church, parishes, dioceses, episcopal conferences or patriarchates.

Everything in the Church, including its teaching, is subject to the word of God which calls it into existence:

> This teaching office is not above the word of God, but serves it, teaching only what has been handed on, listening to it devoutly, guarding it scrupulously and explaining it faithfully in accord with a divine commission and with the help of the Holy Spirit, it draws from this one deposit of faith everything which it presents for belief as divinely revealed.[29]

---

28. Ibid., 45.
29. VATICAN II, *Dei Verbum*, 10.

The Church, therefore, is not like a political community or a business which could change its basic principles and constitution at the behest of the present generation of voters or the existing shareholders. The message of the Gospel and definitively established doctrinal truths are not ours to adapt, nor are they meant only for our time and place. They are a gift of God, learned within the faith community, shared with the whole Church, and intended to be shared with all humanity.

On the other hand, we should never be unwilling to dialogue with those, whether within the Church or outside it, who find difficulty with particular teachings or who cannot accept them. On the contrary, it is the responsibility of the whole community to help make the Gospel known. We cannot do that unless we are willing to make the effort to understand the outlook of those who struggle with their belonging to the Church. We need even to be willing to reach out to those who are hostile to believers and to the very concept of faith. Cardinal Montini, later Paul VI, said to his priests in Milan:

> We will love all those whom we approach and who may have contempt for us, hinder us, perhaps even offend us. But we will never be able to feel offended. The less we are loved the more we will love ... The more difficult it becomes to free the world of its illusions of happiness, self-sufficiency, satisfaction, the more we will love it.[30]

MULTIFACETED COMMUNION
Recent years have provided many examples of the complexity of our relationships and the difficulty of mutual listening and understanding. One difficulty arises from the nature of religious commitment. There is nothing more important than our relationship to God. There are, of course, basic truths which

---

30. MONTINI, G-B., *The Priest*, Dublin: Helicon, 1965, p. 168.

should be defended. However, parish or community meetings discussing legitimate differences about how to proceed may display an intensity that would be justified only if fundamental issues of faith were at stake. No discussion should start from an assumption of malicious ill will on the part of those who take a different view. If we really believed that 'it is often a younger person who knows what is best', and that we should look at every participant knowing that 'in every one of them the Spirit of God breathes', meetings might be both less fraught and more open to what God is asking of us. Working out the pastoral priorities for a parish or group is not a process of each person seeking to ensure that his or her plans are adopted. It is a prayerful process of seeking to be in harmony with God's plan and to be open to the inspiration of the Holy Spirit.

The intensity of the argument in some quarters about the new translation of the *Roman Missal* reflected the fact that liturgy, and especially the Eucharist, is at the heart of our faith. There was a fear that the changed style of language would further discourage people who were already drifting away from regular practice. Whatever one's feelings on the issue, the process of moving from a familiar translation to one with some confusingly minor changes is initially a distraction from the meaning of the prayers.

The really important issue lies deeper than the language. It shows the ease with which the communion which is the essence of the Church can descend into 'them and us'. Even in the most ideal of worlds, no process could be devised to allow millions of people to take part in a consultation about individual wordings. What is unfortunate, in retrospect, is that no way was found for widespread diffusion and discussion of the principles and criteria, as stated in a document of the Congregation for Divine Worship in 2001, according to which the translation was done.[31]

---

31. CONGREGATION FOR DIVINE WORSHIP, *Liturgiam Authenticam* (2001).

There is no conceivable structure which could provide a framework to allow everyone to be actively involved in the details of every decision. That kind of participation will exist only in the new creation where the blessed will see God face to face and 'love one another as themselves, and they will rejoice in the others' good as their own'.[32]

A more painful 'them and us' division was and is evident in the issue of the sexual abuse of children by priests and religious. In this area there are two priorities. The first is recognising and responding to the suffering of those who were abused as children; that has to be paramount. The second priority has to be that everything possible is done to ensure that children are safe.

In the initial years of the emergence of this tragic issue there was a feeling among bishops, and to a lesser extent priests, that this was 'our' problem. This was paralleled by an equally widespread feeling among laity that this was 'their' problem. In spite of the very welcome involvement of volunteers and professionals in shaping the Church response, the challenge has not yet been widely seen for what it is – a matter for the whole communion of the Church as well as for the whole of society.

The roles required, both specialised and non-specialised, are so varied that no one individual or group can adequately fulfil them. There are many competing demands:

- responding to complainants with compassion and readiness to listen;

- offering care and support to the complainant in the long journey towards serenity;

- at the same time not prejudging the accused priest;

---

32. AQUINAS, *Collationes super Credo in Deum*, 12.

- maintaining a pastoral concern while dealing with a complainant's legal claims, which come expressed in the adversarial language of a civil legal process;

- respecting the rights of those whose guilt is not established;

- respecting the rights of those whose guilt has been established – they too have been invited into communion with God and with all humanity, an invitation God never withdraws;

- trying to find the kind of support and supervision for an offender that will minimise the risk of future offences while not seeming in any way to minimise the crime;

- responding to a situation where no allegation has been made but where there may be reasons for concern which cannot be made specific through investigations by the civil authorities or by a Church enquiry;

- dealing with a situation where nothing has been established and nothing is likely to be established;

- recognising that people have a right to expect that no priest who might be an abuser should be sent to a parish;

- recognising that others will protest at what they see as an injustice to the priest whose guilt has not been established and against whom the DPP has decided not to proceed;

- the question of how to treat a person against whom nothing has been established when some degree of suspicion remains: does the presumption of innocence count for anything in such cases?;

❧ recognising that, in the absence of a clear alibi, it is usually impossible to prove a negative.

These and other demands throw up seemingly insoluble issues that need to be widely discussed – yet it is usually impossible to do so in an individual ongoing case. Through the publication of 'Child Sex Abuse: Framework for a Church Response', known as 'The Green Book' (1996), and through continuing developments since that time, a much wider involvement has been brought about. If we as a whole community could at an earlier stage have found ways of looking at these issues – and not only in relation to accusations of abuse by priests, but to the child abuse which affects so many people in society – we might not have had the level of shock and bitterness that we have experienced.

The understandable focus on clerical abuse has masked the realisation of the scale of child abuse in society. The phrase 'One in Four' implies that a horrifying proportion of people are abused as children. The SAVI Report puts the figure slightly lower, at about 17 per cent.[33]

Here surely is something that shows the need for the whole of society to see itself as a community. The Church, which is meant to live as a communion in the life of God, is called to be a sign of what community should be. To live that call means that there should be an attitude of sensitivity, of readiness to listen, of awareness of the need for healing in all of those around us, but in a particular way among those who were so horribly treated as children. It means that the Church should see itself as a home and school of communion for her members and further afield. These issues are important in themselves, but also because they are the basis for challenging people to become

33. McGEE, H., GARAVAN, R., DE BARRA, M., BYRNE, J., CONROY, R., The SAVI Report, Dublin: Royal College of Surgeons, 2002.

more active, more audible, more articulate, seeing their faith as a life in communion.

Any misperception that the communication of the Gospel message, the question of religious vocations, the values that underlie our national life, Catholic education and so on are problems *primarily or perhaps only for the clergy and for the institution* would be disastrous. This has been a weakness in Irish Catholicism, and although this is changing, it remains prevalent. Paradoxically, it is at least partly the fruit of the extraordinary and admirable role played by priests, religious and missionaries in building the identity of the Church in Ireland in past centuries. But it has left the laity far too often 'waiting to be asked', or 'waiting to be told' how they should respond as Christians in the world in which we live.

If (and only if) 'the great forces that shape our world … are guided by people who are true disciples of Christ, and who are, at the same time, fully competent in the relevant secular knowledge and skill, then indeed will the world be transformed from within by Christ's redeeming power'.[34] They can do that, not as isolated individuals, but as members of the Body of Christ, living in the communion of God's life, which is God's gift and promise.

NO COMPLACENCY

Jesus told a parable about two brothers: one agreed to do what his father asked but failed to do so, the other refused but then did what he was asked. At the end of the parable Jesus shocked the chief priests and elders by saying: 'Truly I tell you, the tax-collectors and the prostitutes are going into the kingdom of God ahead of you' (Mt 21:31). Commenting on this, Pope Benedict said to his listeners:

---

34. JOHN PAUL II, Homily in Limerick, 1 October 1979.

Translated into the language of the present day, this statement might sound something like this: agnostics, who are constantly exercised by the question of God, those who long for a pure heart but suffer on account of their sin, are closer to the Kingdom of God than believers whose life of faith is 'routine' and who regard the Church merely as an institution, without letting it touch their hearts, or letting the faith touch their hearts.[35]

The challenge is great. The world badly needs a witness to God's gift of communion. That means courageously recognising where *our* faith has become routine and where *we* look on the Church merely as an institution. The words of Pope John Paul in Ireland need to be heard again: 'Let there be no complacency.'[36]

※

35. BENEDICT XVI, Homily in Freiburg im Breisgau, 25 September 2011.
36. JOHN PAUL II, Address to Priests, Missionaries and Religious, Maynooth, 1 October 1979.

CHAPTER TWO

By Its Very Nature Missionary

WHO IS A MISSIONARY?

THE GREAT MISSIONARY, BISHOP Joseph Shanahan of Southern Nigeria, grew up in the village of Templederry in North Tipperary. He spoke in later life about the deep effect his mother's faith had on him and about the enormous value his father placed on education. That was why he was convinced that education was the most effective way of overcoming slavery in Africa.

After a visit to the tomb of St Thérèse in Lisieux in 1920, the year he became a bishop, he adopted the practice of beginning all his sermons and talks in Ireland with the words, 'My dear fellow missionaries'. He used to explain that 'the missionary's greatest reliance is … on the prayers and sacrifices of those at home who cause [the grace of his priesthood] to be stirred up so powerfully that his contact with the pagans is made very fertile'.[1]

So when he visited his home village, located about fifteen miles from the nearest town of any size, many of whose residents would rarely if ever have travelled the one hundred miles to Dublin or the eighty to Cork, he addressed them as his 'fellow missionaries'.

He was foreshadowing what the Second Vatican Council would declare over forty years later: 'The Church on earth is by its very nature missionary.'[2] The Council spoke about the Holy Spirit 'inspiring in the hearts of the faithful that same spirit of mission which impelled Christ himself'.[3] Those texts point us

---

1. JORDAN, J., *Bishop Shanahan of Southern Nigeria*, Dublin: Elo Press, 1948, p. 187.
2. VATICAN II, *Ad Gentes*, 2.
3. Ibid., 4.

towards one the most fundamental implications of our Christian faith: if we are Christians, we have to be missionaries.

The Council put it clearly: 'All disciples of Christ are obliged to spread the faith to the best of their ability.'[4] It is important that we put everything in the context of this fundamental missionary vocation. From the beginning of the Church, mission was seen as 'the normal outcome of Christian living, to which every believer was committed through the witness of personal conduct and through explicit proclamation whenever possible'.[5] What was being highlighted by Bishop Shanahan was not something new, yet his words were remembered because the truth had slipped out of the centre of people's consciousness. Has it also slipped from ours? Would an objective observer of our daily activities detect any evidence that spreading the faith is a priority in our lives?

'The spirit of a missionary' is the same Spirit which came on the apostles at Pentecost and sent them out to proclaim in all the various languages of the earth the mighty works of God; the same spirit that Bishop Shanahan recognised when he alerted his Irish listeners to the fact that they were his fellow missionaries.

The Gospel he was preaching in Southern Nigeria was the same Gospel that he had heard from the neighbours who surrounded him when he was growing up in Templederry; it was the Gospel that had been lived and celebrated and handed on in that small village for generations by what you might be tempted to call 'ordinary lay people'. It was the same insight that led Pope John Paul to say during his visit to Limerick in 1979 that there is no such thing as an 'ordinary' layperson:

> ... for all of you have been called to conversion through the death and resurrection of Jesus Christ. As God's holy people you are called to fulfil your role in the evangelisation of the world.[6]

---

4. VATICAN II, *Lumen Gentium*, 17.
5. JOHN PAUL II, *Redemptoris Missio*, 27.
6. JOHN PAUL II, Homily in Limerick, 1 October 1979.

More than that, what is at stake here is the realisation that mission is not carried out primarily by individuals, or by missionary societies. It is carried out by whole Christian communities.

In the encyclical on the Church's missionary mandate, Pope John Paul says:

> The early Church experiences her mission as a community task, while acknowledging in her midst certain 'special envoys' or 'missionaries devoted to the Gentiles', such as Paul and Barnabas.[7]

THE RESPONSIBILITY OF ALL

One of the challenges, in the Church in Ireland and elsewhere, is that we are now being brought face to face with the fact that in recent centuries the community had, in many ways, handed over aspects of its responsibility to specialised groups.

The role of religious congregations in education and in health care and in reaching out to the marginalised has been one of the most positive and fruitful elements of the Church's life. But the fruitfulness of those efforts may have led 'ordinary lay people' to think that these aspects of the Church's mission were not their responsibility. There was a similar 'handing over' of the task of evangelisation to 'missionaries'. Bishop Shanahan's use of the phrase 'my fellow missionaries' was not just a tribute to his listeners; it was also an invitation to them to recognise that the work he was doing in Africa was their work and that it was a fruit of their faith.

Something similar can occur with the work of vocations directors, which carries the risk of allowing most members of the Church to think, 'someone else is taking care of all that'. It also happens when liturgical celebration, pastoral care and parish administration are seen as 'the priest's job', as if no one else had any role to play.

---

7. *Redemptoris Missio*, 62.

The strange thing is that, as Bishop Shanahan recognised, the 'handing over' often happened more in theory than in practice. The strength and vibrancy of the faith he lived and preached owed far more to 'ordinary lay people' than they realised. People witnessed to their faith in their own localities, they gave pastoral care to their neighbours in times of need or bereavement or difficulty, they gave help and advice to young parents, they encouraged vocations, and they prayed and gave personal and practical support to their family members who were working on the missions. And that was the context in which young Joseph Shanahan had grown up.

When he later preached to people in Ireland, he was, I suspect, not just trying to create a sense of solidarity with his missionary work, but trying to awaken his congregation to what they were already doing and, in particular, make them aware of its significance in the life of the Church. Things that they took for granted were a vital part of the life of their parish and of the wider Church. Whether they realised it or not, he had been sent out, as thousands of others had been, from towns and villages throughout Ireland. These missionaries were, you might say, 'special envoys' to bring the faith that was nurtured and lived in those parishes to people in Africa, America, Australia and all over the world.

At least half of the task of fostering lay involvement in this as in other areas is to make people aware of the role that what they may consider their 'ordinary' lives *already* play in the Church.

That sense needs to be heightened. Certainly the experience of the diocese of Limerick in recent years has been a growth in the conscientisation of parishes and individuals about the role that they play in the missionary work being done by two of our priests in the outskirts of Lima in Peru and in the work of the St James Society. Sometimes people ask how a diocese in Ireland today, with the sharp decline in vocations, can 'afford' to send priests abroad. This question suggests that it is a kind of a luxury for a parish or a diocese to put resources and efforts into pastoral needs outside itself when its own 'internal' needs are so great. The truth is that the two efforts are mutually enriching and that a parish or diocese which operates on the basis that 'we will take care of ourselves before we think of looking beyond our borders' would be contributing to its own decline.

The role of the Church in relation to mission is two-fold. There is first of all the mission to those who are hearing the Gospel for the first time. But there is also the mission of making the home Church, the Church from which 'foreign' missionaries are sent, more aware of its own missionary character. These two aspects cannot be seen as separate.

In the context of missionary activity, Pope John Paul attaches particular importance to the passage in John's Gospel where Jesus says, 'As you, Father, are in me and I am in you, may they also be in us, so that the world may believe that you have sent me' (Jn 17:21).

> The ultimate purpose of mission is to enable people to share in the communion which exists between the Father and the Son. The disciples are to live in unity with one another, remaining in the Father and the Son, so that the world may know and believe (cf. Jn 17:21-23). This is a very important missionary text. It makes us understand that we are missionaries above all because of *what we are* as a Church whose inmost life is unity in love, even before we become missionaries in *word or deed*.[8]

The home Church has nurtured the faith of the missionary in the first place and has given him/her the urge to enable other people to share in the richness of communion in God's life. And the life

---

8.   Ibid., 23 (italics in original).

of the home Church is deepened and expanded by the work of
the missionary:

> For missionary activity renews the Church, revitalises faith
> and Christian identity, and offers fresh enthusiasm and new
> incentives. *Faith is strengthened when it is given to others!* [9]

There is a kind of mutuality between the primordial vocation
received by the missionary and the enrichment which that
community receives through the flourishing of that vocation in
the many different contexts in which it is lived out, whether at
home or abroad.

ALL IS GIFT

There are a number of ways in which we can distort the meaning
of that primordial vocation. One of them is our instinctive
reaction when we hear that all disciples of Christ are *obliged* to be
missionaries. We live in an era where the concept of obligation is
problematic. Our culture is hardwired to react to any suggestion
of an obligation by thinking, 'Who are you to tell me what I have
to do?'

In speaking about the apparently unrelated question of social
morality, Pope Benedict introduced a new principle which he
called 'the principle of gratuitousness'. The English translation
is, to say the least, inelegant. The principle is, however, simply a
recognition of the fundamental fact of creation and redemption
that *everything is gift; everything is grace.*

> As the absolutely gratuitous gift of God, hope bursts into our
> lives as something not due to us, something that transcends
> every law of justice. Gift by its nature goes beyond merit,
> its rule is that of superabundance. It takes first place in our

---

9. Ibid., 2 (italics in original).

souls as a sign of God's presence in us, a sign of what he expects from us ... The unity of the human race, a fraternal communion transcending every barrier, is called into being by the word of God-who-is-Love ... economic, social and political development, if it is to be authentically human, needs to make room for the *principle of gratuitousness* as an expression of fraternity.[10]

The unity of the human race is founded on God's gift and it should express itself in solidarity. In *Sollicitudo Rei Socialis*, Pope John Paul described solidarity, which, he says, is 'undoubtedly a Christian virtue'.[11] He returns to this concept in *Evangelium Vitae*:

> *Solidarity* helps us to see the 'other' ... as our 'neighbour' ... to be made a sharer, on a par with ourselves, in the banquet of life to which all are equally invited by God.[12]

The kind of obligation that is involved in answering the call of God-who-is-love is not some kind of external coercion. It makes sense only in the context of the fundamental, superabundant gift – 'In this is love: not that we have loved God, but that he loved us and sent his Son as expiation for our sins' (I Jn 4:10). The superabundance of God's gift is symbolised in the first of Jesus' signs, at Cana, where the wedding party had celebrated longer and better than the couple had expected. Christ gave his first sign, a sign of the nature of God's love by providing them not with a few bottles to tide them over an embarrassing moment, but with something in the region of *150 gallons* of the best wine.

---

10. BENEDICT XVI, *Caritas in Veritate*, 34 (italics in original).
11. JOHN PAUL II, *Sollicitudo Rei Socialis*, 40.
12. Ibid., 39 (my italics). 'Que l'on doit faire participer, à parité avec nous.'

KEEPING OPEN THE DOOR OF FAITH

Sometimes we experience our lives as a burden. But the struggle is not against some outside force that is compelling us to do what is against our own yearnings; it is a struggle with a call that comes from deep within ourselves, a call to persevere in our response to God's infinite love which is the source of meaning for our lives; it is a free response for the sake of our own fidelity to the gift and call we have received.

Viewing obligation as something imposed on us from outside, rather than as our own effort to respond to the unimaginable generosity of God, has distorted people's understanding of Christianity 'poured into our hearts' in all sorts of ways. How many of us, when the going is tough, can recite Psalm 118 (119) and really mean it? It consists of almost two hundred verses, and in a variety of different ways each of them says that God's commandments, God's law, God's will, God's demands are marvellous, delightful, better than silver and gold.

The fundamental missionary obligation is not something added to the Good News as a burden or an inconvenience. It is simply the overflowing of that sense that what we have received is both so wonderful and so inexhaustible that we feel the obligation to share it. As Peter and John said to the high priests and rulers, 'We cannot but speak of what we have seen and heard' (Acts 4:20).

Pope John Paul spoke of how the Christian should perceive the obligations of following Christ:

> ... those who are impelled by love and 'walk by the Spirit' (Gal 5:16), and who desire to serve others, find in God's Law the fundamental and necessary way in which to practise love as something *freely chosen and freely lived out*. Indeed, they feel an interior urge – a genuine 'necessity' and no longer a form of coercion – not to stop at the minimum demands of the Law, but to live them in their 'fullness'.[13]

---

13. JOHN PAUL II, *Veritatis Splendor*, 18 (my italics).

The obligation is, first of all, one that emerges from within, from a heart that is responding to the implications of a gift recognised and freely responded to.

In responding to the question of why the whole Church and each member of it should be missionary therefore, we need to begin with that internal motivation. Its meaning is to be a love 'freely chosen and freely lived out'. Wherever we are and whatever the circumstances of our lives, each of us is called to be missionary as part of the original mission of our baptism and confirmation, which is the 'normal outcome' of being a Christian believer.

TENSIONS AND OPPORTUNITIES

It may be normal, but it is not easy! There is a somewhat confused tradition according to which the old Irish monks referred to missionary exile as 'white martyrdom'. In a sense, however, every Christian is an exile because he or she is in the process of bringing the Gospel to the new continent of the contemporary world in which the Gospel has never been lived or spoken before.

One of the tensions of mission fields in the past has been the scandal of Christian divisions. In what is, thank God, an age of ecumenism, the scandal of fierce competition between Christian churches on the mission field is greatly diminished, at least between the mainstream churches. Of course tensions remain about proselytism and the improper use of money from richer countries to entice people and so on, or to provide for them in a way that risks diminishing their own initiative and responsibility. There is also the difficulty that arises because not all Christian groups are committed to an ecumenical outlook.

We have to approach these tensions with the awareness that Christian divisions damage the work of mission, that our own history is not free of reproach, that the aim of our work cannot be to defeat fellow Christians but, to the best of our ability and to the greatest extent possible, to seek unity with them. Some sects and groups can create difficulties for the Catholic Church and for other Christian communities, but the aim, according to *Redemptoris Missio*, is that 'wherever possible and in the light of local circumstances, the response of Christians can be an ecumenical one'.[14]

Another way in which that primordial vocation can be distorted is by seeing it as some kind of permission to regard oneself as superior, to see oneself as bringing something to people who one feels are in some way inferior to oneself. The fear that we may be perceived as imposing or as feeling superior has, I believe, caused a great deal of heart-searching among missionaries. So too has the question of how to respond to non-Christian religions.

The Second Vatican Council recognised the value of other religions:

> The Catholic Church rejects nothing of what is true and holy in these religions. It has a high regard for the manner of life and conduct, the precepts and doctrines which, although differing in many aspects from its own teaching, nonetheless often reflect a ray of that Truth which enlightens all men and women.[15]

The Vatican Council also taught that the Holy Spirit offers to all people of good will, even those who do not believe at all, 'the possibility of being made partners in a way known to God, in the paschal mystery'.[16]

Some of the rhetoric surrounding the missions in the past seemed to pay insufficient attention to that universality of God's grace. Pope Benedict XV played an enlightened part in seeking to end the First World War. He wrote an Apostolic Letter about the

---

14. *Redemptoris Missio*, 50.
15. VATICAN II, *Nostra Aetate*, 2.
16. VATICAN II, *Gaudium et Spes*, 22.

activity of missionaries. Having talked about the importance of relieving poverty, however, he added:

> How much more then should one observe the holy law of charity when it is a matter not just of helping an unlimited number of people who are living between misery and hunger, but also and principally a matter of snatching a huge multitude of souls from slavery to Satan in order to win them for the freedom of the sons of God?[17]

Obviously it is true that the most important gift that anyone could offer to another human being would be to open them up to receive the freedom of God's children. But we have rightly become very uneasy about any suggestion that those who have not heard the Gospel and who are not baptised are doomed to live and die in slavery to Satan! On the contrary, we believe that the grace of God is universal and that God wills the salvation of all (1 Tm 2:4).

But this appears to take the urgency out of the missionary imperative. Many older missionaries did see themselves in a rather uncomplicated way as 'snatching souls from slavery to Satan'. When one looks at the children and their parents struggling to live with dignity on the hillsides and suburbs around Lima, or in parts of Africa which have been plagued by famine and even genocide, one hardly begins the missionary project by thinking of them as people who are enslaved by the devil.

SHARING WHAT WE HAVE RECEIVED

We might feel rather more like the Dominican priest described in the book *Angela's Ashes*, who, when the young Frank McCourt confessed that he had stolen a loaf of bread because he was starving, replied, 'My child, I sit here, I hear the sins of the poor. I

---

17. BENEDICT XV, *Maximum Illud* (1919).

assign the penance, I bestow absolution. I should be on my knees washing their feet. Do you understand me, my child?'[18]

The instinct that tells us we should not approach others from a perspective of superiority is entirely correct. This was put very profoundly by the French Catholic philosopher, Gabriel Marcel, in a collection of essays called *Homo Viator*.

> The Christian in fact cannot in any way think of himself as possessing either a power or even an advantage which has been denied to the unbeliever. There we have one of the most paradoxical aspects of his situation, for in another sense, he is obliged to recognise that grace has been bestowed on him. This, however, only remains true on condition that the grace should inhabit him, not only as radiance, but as humility. From the moment he begins to be proud of it as a possession it changes its nature, and I should be tempted to say it becomes a malediction.[19]

There would be an enormous contradiction if one were to envisage a Christian missionary who approached unbelievers with the perspective of the Pharisee, thanking God that he or she is not like the rest of humanity. So how then should we envisage the situation where we have received the gift of Christian, Catholic, faith and others have not?

First of all there is the principle that what we have received is totally gift. Therefore, as in the context in which Pope Benedict XVI uses the concept of gift, nobody has any grounds for feeling superior to others. The logic of possessing and owning and entitlement do not apply. The logic of God is about superabundant gift. The gift of God's love and hope 'bursts into our lives as something not due to us'. It is a gift infinitely beyond

18. McCOURT, F. *Angela's Ashes,* New York: Scribner, 1996, p. 185.
19. MARCEL, G., *Homo Viator,* tr. E. Craufurd, New York, 1962, p. 159.

our ability to achieve or to create. Unless we understand that, we are in no position to communicate it to anyone else. Thus humility is a fundamental requirement of mission. In the name of that humility, Marcel says that a Christian must be constantly on guard against the temptation to paternalism.[20]

But it is even more fundamental than this. In bringing the knowledge of the Gospel to another person, we are in a sense bringing them what they already have, or, to put it a different way, we are bringing them the knowledge of who they already are.

> All that we can propose to ourselves is, in the last analysis, to awaken within another the consciousness of what he is, or, more precisely, of his divine filiation, to teach him to see himself as the child of God through the love which is shown him ... But in reality I do not give or bring him anything. I merely direct the adoration of which God is the unique object on to the divine life as seen in this creature, who from the beginning has been unaware of his true nature ...[21]

In other words, when we change our perspective to think in terms of 'gratuitousness', we are no longer thinking in terms of something possessed and handed over but in terms of a gift which no human being can earn or control but can only gratefully recognise in oneself and in others.

But this seems to make the question even more acute. If people can be saved anyway and if they are already children of God, what is the point of missionary activity?

INVITED INTO DIALOGUE WITH GOD

Once again, we need to return to the gift. Mission begins where

---

20. Ibid., p. 159.
21. Ibid., p. 160.

every human life begins, from the word of God. It is a teaching of the Catholic Church that 'every spiritual soul is immediately created by God'.[22] I think this is best understood by putting it like this: the first moment of each human person's existence involves him or her being addressed and invited by God into a relationship. One might say that in the beginning of each of our lives, God says, 'Let there be you'. *Gaudium et Spes* says that 'This invitation to converse with God is addressed to man [or woman] as soon as he comes into being.'[23]

That is the most profound meaning of personhood. In his reflection on the Word of God, Pope Benedict speaks of how God's love bridges the gap between Creator and creature and brings about a relationship of love:

> In this vision every man and woman appears as someone to whom the word speaks, challenges and calls to enter this dialogue of love through a free response. Each of us is thus enabled by God to hear and respond to his word. We were created in the word and we live in the word; we cannot understand ourselves unless we are open to this dialogue. The word of God discloses the filial and relational nature of human existence.[24]

Mission is about enabling people to understand more fully the significance of that word which God speaks in the depth of every human heart. But this means that mission has to be about a relationship in which people meet as people. It has to be a relationship where, in the words of Blessed John Henry Newman's motto, 'Heart speaks to heart'. It has to become part of that dialogue.

---

22. *Catechism of the Catholic Church*, 366; cf. Fifth Lateran Council DS 1440.
23. *Gaudium et Spes*, 19. ('Ad colloquium cum Deo iam inde ab ortu suo invitatur homo.')
24. BENEDICT XVI, *Verbum Domini*, 22.

The documents of the Pontifical Council for Interreligious Dialogue speak about the relationship between proclamation and dialogue.[25] Dialogue involves four areas.

There is *a dialogue of life* in which people share life-experience of joys, sorrows, problems and preoccupations. There is *a dialogue of action* in which Christians work together with others for the freedom and well-being of people. There is *a dialogue of religious experience* in which people share their own religious traditions and its richness and share their search for God. There is also a fourth form, which is usually a more specialised area – *a dialogue of theological exchange.*[26] To say that formal theological dialogue is a specialised area does not mean that what we wrongly call 'ordinary lay people' should have no element of what we used to call apologetics. They should be able to explain, for instance, that we do not worship statues, and to say that we do recognise the primacy of God's love and that everything is gift.[27] Nevertheless there is an important area of professional theological dialogue which requires a certain expertise and which is found especially in formal dialogue between Christian traditions. None of the dimensions of dialogue are optional extras:

> On the contrary, guided by the Pope and their bishops, all local Churches, and all members of these Churches are called to dialogue though not all in the same way.[28]

The various forms of dialogue clearly interact. The dialogue of life, namely a readiness to share the joys and sorrows of

---

25. PONTIFICAL COUNCIL FOR INTER-RELIGIOUS DIALOGUE, *Dialogue and Mission* (1984), *Dialogue and Proclamation* (1991).

26. See *Dialogue and Proclamation*, 42.

27. 'By grace alone, in faith in Christ's saving work and not because of any merit on our part, we are accepted by God and receive the Holy Spirit, who renews our hearts while equipping and calling us to good works.' Joint Declaration on the Doctrine of Justification by the Lutheran World Federation and the Catholic Church, n. 15.

28. *Dialogue and Proclamation*, 42.

other human beings, is a basic requirement of any missionary endeavour; so too is a willingness to address along with others the problems and sufferings and needs of society. This should, as Father Donal Dorr puts it, lead to making 'a serious attempt to understand and respect each other's religious beliefs, values, rituals and organisation'.[29] Ideally, it should lead on not just to a sharing about faith, but, to whatever extent possible, a sharing of faith where our search for God is enriched by theirs. Blessed John Paul wrote: 'One may define the human being, therefore, as the one who seeks the truth.'[30] And that search is ultimately a search for God. As Pope John Paul wrote elsewhere: 'Objectively speaking, the search for truth and the search for God are one and the same.'[31]

HEART SPEAKS TO HEART

What is at stake here, it seems to me, is that the word of God can only be spoken effectively and evangelisation can only take place if people are addressed heart to heart. It can only happen if they are touched at the point where the deeper questions are asked. But that requires sharing and understanding their joys and sorrows, their struggles, and the religious tradition in which they seek to address the questions of life and meaning and the search for peace and justice and truth and love. And it demands sharing those questions and struggles, not just from some ivory tower, but as one who genuinely feels them.

To say that we reject nothing that is true and holy in other religions means that we have to take them seriously. We must not see them just as obstacles or as competitors but as contexts in which our fellow human beings meet God. They are the space in which they encounter God's search for them. In every religious tradition – and some are richer than others – there is a search for

29. DORR, D., *Mission in Today's World,* Dublin: Columba Press, 2000, p. 21.
30. JOHN PAUL II, *Fides et Ratio*, 28.
31. JOHN PAUL II, Message for the World Day of Peace, 1991, Section II.

ultimate truth and meaning. There is nothing more sacred in any human life than that search for God. That is the search to which the Good News speaks.

If we understand the importance of the other person's search, we will want to give them some insight into how the richness and the truth of the Catholic tradition give meaning and hope to our lives.

Maybe at this point we are back to Bishop Shanahan. His faith grew not, I suspect, in the sermons he heard in the parish church, nor in the theology books he read in the seminary. It grew because he was in contact with the hearts of his mother and father and his neighbours, because he met priests and religious and lay people who touched his heart with their faith. He was in touch with them in their joys and sorrows and in touch with how all that life brought them was seen in the light of their faith. Christianity is not, as Pope Benedict put it in the first page of his first encyclical, a theory but an encounter with a person 'which gives life a new horizon and a decisive direction'.[32] And that encounter with Christ took place inseparably from his encounter with the people of his home parish.

The reality is that when people meet in that kind of 'real' human relationship, when they truly share life's experiences and challenges, there is nothing more natural than that they begin to share what life means to them; they share how they face the problems, how they continue to hope. This mutual recognition, understanding and respect often begins without putting it into words.

In a lot of modern western life, that is not the way people meet. Their encounters outside their own families and close friends – even tragically sometimes within their own families – are remote, cold, anonymous, steering clear of what are thought of as 'divisive' religious questions.

---

32. BENEDICT XVI, *Deus Caritas Est*, 1.

The truth is that in seeking the answers to these questions, heart speaks to heart. We find in other people an echo of our own search for beauty and truth and unity and meaning. Our dialogue leads towards the chief aim of communication:

> In the Christian faith, human unity and brotherhood are the chief aims of all communication and these find their source and model in the central mystery of the eternal communion between the Father, Son and Holy Spirit who live a single divine life.[33]

Therefore the transition from dialogue to mission is imperceptible. Mission has already begun, and it has to begin, in the love and respect for the other person before there is any explicit proclamation of the word.

The answer to the question 'why mission?' becomes evident every time we recognise in another person an echo of the same word which spoke to our hearts at the beginning of our existence and throughout our life in a Christian family and in the various Christian communities in which we have lived and worked. In that recognition, heart already speaks to heart.

MISSION IN IRELAND TODAY

How stands the concept of mission in Ireland today? It is a question we would not have thought necessary when the Second Vatican Council opened fifty years ago.

We were well aware that we had an extraordinary missionary tradition. Almost every town and village, and most families, could boast that they had their own missionaries working in faraway parts of the world. It was something to be proud of. However, the very success of that effort may have led to a certain complacency.

---

33. *Communio et Progressio*, 8.

When one looks back at the first three-quarters of the twentieth century, one can only be struck by the vibrancy of the Irish missionary movement, the high Mass attendance, the crowded seminaries and the central role of the Church in society. Perhaps this left us reluctant to believe that we had much to learn from places like 'the continent', where faith seemed to be struggling.

Consequently we failed to learn the lessons that we needed to learn; and when the same issues began to strike at home, we floundered. We were not, and perhaps are still not, willing to do the hard thinking and to accept the renewal required by the documents and insights of Vatican II, by the challenges of the intervening years and to accept the pain of facing up to the real challenges of our present situation.

For instance, how strong is the conviction among most Irish parishioners that Pope John Paul's words apply to each of them as individuals and as a community and pose clear challenges to them?

> The need for all the faithful to share in this [missionary] responsibility is not merely a matter of making the apostolate more effective, it is a right and duty based on their baptismal dignity, whereby 'the faithful participate, for their part, in the threefold mission of Christ as Priest, Prophet and King'. Therefore, 'they are bound by the general obligation and they have the right, whether as individuals or in associations, to strive so that the divine message of salvation may be known and accepted by all people throughout the world. This obligation is all the more insistent in circumstances in which only through them are people able to hear the Gospel and to know Christ.' Furthermore, because of their secular character, they especially are called 'to seek the kingdom of God by engaging in temporal affairs and ordering these in accordance with the will of God'.[34]

---

34. *Redemptoris Missio*, 72.

'The missionary thrust ... belongs to the very nature of the Christian life ...'[35] Without that missionary thrust, in other words, something essential is missing from the Christian life of any parish or diocese. We can identify symptoms of what is weak or missing, for instance:

- the sense of possessing a gift which, if we have even begun to understand it, we are driven to share;

- the awareness that this obligation is all-pervasive, applying in every part of our lives and at all times, and a sense of urgency about the effort to communicate the Good News;

- the sense of thankfulness which sees everything as gift and which knows that in our faith we have a treasure which we have in no way deserved or earned;

- the sense of sin as an offence not only against God but against God's people and the witness we are called to give;

- the realisation that we are a community which by charity, example and prayer is meant to be seeking the conversion of sinners (including ourselves!)[36] – in other words that we bear a responsibility for one another's Christian lives;

- the sense of being involved together in the universal priesthood and hence of being a community with common calling and purpose to 'teach all nations', to consecrate the world to God and to offer it to God when we are called together (*ecclesia*) to celebrate the liturgy.

---

35. Ibid., 1.
36. See *Lumen Gentium*, 11.

None of this implies an insensitive and arrogant imposition of one's views on others. It is first of all a respectful encounter with others. Pope Benedict expresses it well:

> A Christian knows when it is time to speak of God and when it is better to say nothing and to let love alone speak. He knows that God is love (cf. 1 Jn 4:8) and that God's presence is felt at the very time when the only thing we do is to love.[37]

It is not enough that there should be many individuals and groups in the parish who to a greater or lesser extent recognise their missionary role; what is needed is an understanding that this is a defining characteristic of the parish (and of the diocese and of the universal Church) itself.

It is the role of the parish to be a welcoming family home 'where those who have been baptised and confirmed become aware of forming the People of God ... from that home they are sent out day by day to their apostolic mission in all the centres of activity of the life of the world'.[38]

We are a people who are not called just as individuals; we are brought together as a single people;[39] all baptised people are called together in one flock and bear united witness to one faith.[40]

There is of course no magic wand which will transform a parish into a self-aware, dynamic, missionary unit overnight! We need to think not just in terms of programmes run by the clergy or the diocese, but also of small groups of parishioners who have reflected and prayed and learned, and who are willing to take on the challenge of awakening the 'sleeping giant' of the parish or diocese.

---

37. *Deus Caritas Est*, 31 c.
38. *Catechesi Tradendae*, 67.
39. See *Lumen Gentium*, 9.
40. See *Ad Gentes*, 6.

CHAPTER THREE

The Noble Obligation

A NEW CONTINENT

THE SECOND VATICAN COUNCIL called on lay people, whoever they are, 'to expend all their energy for the growth of the Church and its continuous sanctification ...'[1]

In the organism of a living body, no member is purely passive: sharing in the life of the body each member also shares in its activity. The same is true in the body of Christ, which is the Church: the whole body, 'when each part is working properly, promotes the body's growth' (Eph 4:16).[2]

> On all Christians, accordingly, rests the noble obligation of bringing all people the whole world over to hear and accept the divine message of salvation.[3]

Pope John Paul spoke words in Knock which have always echoed in my mind. I don't think that we have ever fully taken on board how central they are for the Church of our time and the challenge that they pose for every member of the Church today. He said:

> [T]he task of renewal in Christ is never finished. Every generation, with its own mentality and characteristics, is like a new continent to be won for Christ. The Church must constantly look for new ways that will enable her to understand more profoundly and to carry out with renewed vigour the mission received from her Founder.[4]

---

1. VATICAN II, *Lumen Gentium,* Dogmatic Constitution on the Church, 33.
2. VATICAN II, *Apostolicam Actuositatem*, Decree on the Laity, 2.
3. Ibid., 3.
4. JOHN PAUL II, Homily in Knock, 30 September 1979.

The new mentality and characteristics of each generation form a new continent to be 'won for Christ'. What does that concretely mean for us? What are the new 'mentality and characteristics' that we have to take into account? It would be impossible to list them all. A few examples point to some of the huge changes that are occurring in our time and which have transformed the world since the time of Vatican II:

a) We live in a world where communication is changing so rapidly that it is hard to keep up. Increasing numbers of people carry a smart phone by which they are permanently available to other people, even people on other continents, by phone or email; by which they have permanent access to the internet, by which they can access social networks, radio, television and newspapers; on which they can play hundreds of games, and which provides them with a camera from which they can send still and video pictures instantly to anyone or upload them to YouTube for all the world to view; and on which they can download vast amounts of music, video and data of all kind. All of that, which has become commonplace, would have been unimaginable before the beginnings of the World Wide Web less than twenty-five years ago.[5] One can only wonder what developments will have occurred a couple of decades from now.

b) The phenomenon of globalisation means that a crisis in any part of the world now affects everybody almost immediately. There is greater movement of people, goods, capital and ideas. Increased trade and investment across borders make us more interdependent than has ever been the case in the past. All of this might lead to a more united world but it is also possible for it to make us more vulnerable to those who are stronger than we are – and to make us more capable of exploiting those who are weaker.

c) Western Europe, to a degree virtually unknown in history apart from the atheistic dictatorships of the last century,

---

5. Generally dated to a proposal by Sir Tim Berners-Lee in March 1989.

functions in its politics, economics and social structures with little or no reference to God – a world, as someone put it, where God is missing but not missed, a world where most aspects of life are conducted as though God did not exist. Eastern Europe, including countries which are now our fellow members of the European Union, endured a more explicit and more aggressive form of atheistic society for almost fifty years.

d) Climate change and pollution and the voracious appetite for energy may seriously affect the planet itself and how able it will be in the future to foster the flourishing of human life. In the past, the earth's resources seemed inexhaustible.

e) All sorts of new possibilities, promising and terrifying, are arising, and will do so increasingly – the therapeutic potential of adult stem cells, the genetic modification of human beings, the exploration of space. Who can foretell what research in the extraordinary world of nanotechnology will yield? Speculation about future developments is almost pointless as there will inevitably be discoveries and therapeutic interventions we have not even imagined.

f) We are flooded with facts, on the Internet and in the conventional media. No generation has been as aware of events in the world and has had such immediate access to them. But we often feel swamped by this information, and we often have no way of knowing how accurate or how selective it is. Even in simpler days people would commonly remark that whenever you saw a story published in the papers about which you knew the facts, the report was almost always wrong in important details. The sheer scale of news gathering today vastly increases the possibility of an element of news manufacturing. One would want to be fairly naive to imagine that what emerged in Britain during the summer of 2011 was confined to *The News of the World*, or indeed to the British tabloids – or to Britain. The ever-increasing pressure and immediacy of news nowadays makes such distortions and cutting of corners almost inevitable. And how can a responsible journalist in an area of conflict be sure that the information he or she is receiving, or is allowed to receive, is reliable?

g) We live at a time which increasingly looks like an enormous turning point in history, and especially in the history of western civilisation. Desmond Fennell recently wrote about what he called 'the end of western civilisation'. The West, in the last century or so, saw three efforts at radical change – the communist revolution, the growth of fascism, and the liberal-capitalist approach, with enormous multinational companies often more powerful than states. He says that the situation we now find ourselves in is that all three have failed:

> Those three efforts viewed together, each of them supported by millions of people, indicated a strong conviction among twentieth century Europeans, in Europe and overseas, that the civilisation which their ancestors created, and which had enabled them to dominate and lead the world, had ended its usefulness – had had its day ...
>
> The period since then, and continuing ahead of us beyond the collapse of the American liberal utopia, future historians will call 'transitional' and compare it to the transitional period between the civilisations of ancient Rome and Europe ... It will end in a new civilisation, or civilisations, in the West.[6]

These and so many other aspects of our generation add up to 'a new continent to be won for Christ'. The reason is clear – no Christian, no human being, has ever lived in this kind of world before. It is a world in which the Gospel has not yet been preached or lived, or to put it another way, it is a new continent, a foreign mission field.

---

6. FENNELL, D., *Ireland After the End of Western Civilisation*, Belfast: Athol Books, 2009, p. 25. For an updated version, see: http://desmondfennell.com/essay-staggered-end-western-civilisation.htm.

How do we live as Christians in responding to this new world with all its unprecedented potential and risk? Pope John Paul rightly saw that the new mentality and characteristics of this new continent required what he called 'new ways' to communicate the Good News. The truth of his words has become unmistakeably clear in the intervening years.

THE CHOSEN RACE

How to respond as Christians to this new continent became a great theme of Pope John Paul's papacy. This is an inescapable priority in our new continent.

Pope John Paul spelled out the implications of this challenge for every Christian very early in his pontificate, notably during his homily in Limerick. He emphasised the place of lay people in responding to the challenge. What he said is worth quoting at some length:

> Sometimes, lay men and women do not seem to appreciate to the full the dignity and the vocation that is theirs as lay people. No, there is no such thing as an 'ordinary layman', for all of you have been called to conversion through the death and Resurrection of Jesus Christ. *As God's holy people you are called to fulfil your role in the evangelization of the world.*
>
> Yes, the laity are 'a chosen race', 'a holy priesthood', also called to be 'the salt of the earth' and 'the light of the world'. It is their specific vocation and mission *to express the Gospel in their lives and thereby to insert the Gospel as a leaven into the reality of the world in which they live and work.* The great forces which shape the world – politics, the mass media, science, technology, culture, education, industry and work – are precisely the areas where lay people are especially competent to exercise their mission. If these forces are guided by people

who are true disciples of Christ, and who are, at the same time, fully competent in the relevant secular knowledge and skill, then indeed will the world be transformed from within by Christ's redeeming power.[7]

Perhaps one of the most obvious characteristics of the world we live in is its complexity. Nobody could pretend to be an expert in all the vast explosion of knowledge that has occurred in recent centuries. The fifteenth-century Italian philosopher Giovanni Pico della Mirandola was alleged to have challenged all comers to debate with him on the topic, *De omni re scibili* (about everything that can be known). Even then, this was perceived to be a bit ridiculous, and someone added the phrase *et de quibusdam aliis* so that the topic now read 'about everything that can be known – and a few other things as well'! It is certainly clear to us, in a way that might not have been so evident to Giovanni, that nobody can be an expert in everything.

It was always the case that the Christian home, 'the domestic church',[8] was the first and most important field for the sharing of the Gospel. It was the case for many centuries that the popular traditions of piety, of pilgrimages, of holy wells and pattern days gave life to faith in Ireland without necessarily having enthusiastic support from the clergy. What is clear in any case is that the task of bringing the Gospel to bear on the list of spheres outlined in Pope John Paul's Limerick homily has to be carried out by people who are fully competent and involved. The people who can make the Gospel heard in the media are Christian journalists. The people who can make the Gospel heard in politics are Christian politicians. They cannot, of course, fulfil that role if, like a minister in the last Irish government, they believe it is important

---

7.   JOHN PAUL II, Homily in Limerick, 1 October 1979 (my italics). See also similar words written by Pope Paul VI in *Evangelii Nuntiandi*, 70, quoted in *Christifideles Laici*, 23.

8.   *Lumen Gentium*, 11.

to leave their religion outside the door when engaging in politics! The role of bringing the Gospel to bear on industry and finance and economics belongs to Christian workers, business people, economists and politicians.

If something is heard as the voice of 'the Church', it may be regarded as a voice coming from outside these professional and technical spheres. Such interventions are often condescendingly labelled 'the position of those with religious views which of course must be respected'. This usually amounts to a polite and apparently tolerant way of saying that they may be ignored. At best the 'Christian voice' will be seen as expressing some fine ideals, but as distorted by religious belief and as failing to appreciate the complexities involved.

That does not mean, of course, that Catholics should base our arguments on the authority of scripture or papal encyclicals when we speak in the public arena about matters affecting the wider society. That would simply give those who do not believe in Catholic or Christian faith reason to assume that the points being made with such arguments are not relevant to them.

The issue at stake in these spheres is precisely that of human dignity, the common good, issues on which Christians, as Vatican II put it, 'are joined to others in the search for truth, and for the right solution to so many problems that arise both in the life of individuals and from social relationships'.[9] Working out what precise policies and programmes can best foster the common good is a complicated matter on which concerned and responsible people will disagree.

The teaching of the Church does not provide ready-made answers to economic or political questions. The role of faith is different; it is 'to contribute to the purification of reason and to the reawakening of those moral forces without which just structures

---

9. VATICAN II, *Gaudium et Spes,* 16.

are neither established nor prove effective in the long run'.[10] In other words, faith sharpens our perception of basic truths such as the dignity of all human beings and the unity of the human race and thus challenges our complacency. It also intensifies our commitment and our sense of urgency in addressing issues. It gives us a sense of hope because it assures us that life is not absurd and the world is in the hands of God who is infinite love.

We should not disguise the fact that we find inspiration and clarity about who we are and how we should relate to each other from our faith. We should recognise that people of other faiths, and honest searchers for the truth, also find in their understanding of life the energy that drives their commitment to the common good.

This is not a recipe for Christians to regard others as inferior. While recognising and welcoming the contribution of many non-believers to social justice and to the life of the community, we should not disguise the influence that faith can and does have on every aspect of our lives. People who are inspired by a secularist world view generally have no inhibitions about saying so. Why should religious people be embarrassed about their faith?

SOLIDARITY AND COMMUNITY

But let us not be too quick to complain. We need first to acknowledge that believers too can frequently detach the sacred sphere from the secular. We can be tempted, for instance, to see the Mass as a moment when we turn aside from the journey of life to refresh ourselves. It is not by turning aside from life that the Eucharist refreshes us, but by leading us more fully into the deepest meaning of life.

We all accept in theory that the Eucharist is closely related to the world. But it is not enough to accept it in theory. The Eucharist is the 'summit and source' of our lives. It gets to the heart of the

---

10. BENEDICT XVI, *Deus Caritas Est*, 29.

meaning of human life and every aspect and moment of life. Far from being irrelevant to concerns about society, it is at the heart of every reality, including the economy, politics, education, the media, science, technology and culture. 'Everything that can be known and a few other things as well' find their meaning in the mystery which the Eucharist makes present!

The premise of the film *The Matrix* is that what people think of as reality is in fact a computer-generated illusion. Morpheus, the leader of the small group who know the truth, welcomes Neo into their group with the words, 'Welcome to the real world'.

Cardinal Scola referred to that scene in a talk on the Eucharist. The Eucharist, he says, is making a statement: 'This is the heart of reality; this is the meaning of what is real. Welcome to the real world.' 'Welcome' in English and many languages, *bienvenu, benvenuto, willkommen*, means 'It is good that you have come':

> It is good that you, Neo, have entered in the real world: it is good for you, and it is good for us! Is not this the meaning of a mother's first smiles to her baby? Smiles that they learn to reciprocate. What do these smiles mean if not 'it's great that you came to the (real) world; it is good for you, it is good for everyone'? No one escapes this experience.[11]

The Eucharist celebrates the life, death and resurrection of the Word through whom all things were made and in whom all things exist. It celebrates his entry into the human family in the Incarnation, and into the creation which came into being through him. It celebrates his entry through his death and rising, as the first born of the new humanity, into the *new* creation where, without exception, everything that is worthwhile in this life 'will be found again ... illuminated and transfigured',[12] freed from all

---

11.   See Address of Cardinal Scola, at the 31st Meeting of *Comunione e Liberazione*, Rimini, 2010.
12.   *Gaudium et Spes*, 39.

imperfection and vulnerability. And so it *welcomes* all who share in it into the real world of the new creation and into communion with Christ and with one another. It echoes God's first smile to us.

So how can our faith be irrelevant to anything in creation or to any sphere of life? If it is seen as irrelevant to these things, sometimes perhaps even by ourselves, that is a profound failure to understand and communicate our faith.

'GOD HAS AS IT WERE DISAPPEARED'

There is a kind of deafness or blindness about life today. Life does not seem to leave room for talking about God. When theologians or preachers talk about salvation or redemption or grace, what echo, if any, do such words have in people's lives? If they have no echo, is that because the words have lost their meaning, or is it because people rarely think in terms of the dimension of life to which the words refer? Pope John Paul described this deafness well:

> One might say that there are fewer declared atheists, but more non-believers, people who live as though God did not exist and who place themselves outside the question of faith versus unbelief. God has, as it were, disappeared from their existential horizon.[13]

There is an almost inescapable tendency to divide modern life into compartments – economics, politics, technology, art and religion etc. But the *whole point* about religion, about religious faith, is that *it is not a compartment;* it concerns the whole of life.

When we feel that society is becoming more secularist, it doesn't necessarily mean that an aggressive anti-religious atheism is taking over. There is a far less aggressive, and far more

---

13. JOHN PAUL II, to the Secretariat for Non-Believers, 5 March 1988.

insidious, form of secularism. This says that religion is fine so long as it keeps to its place, recognises that it is a private matter, does not intrude into the public arena and does not engage in embarrassing manifestations of personal beliefs; it must especially avoid any suggestion that such beliefs have anything to do with commitment to and understanding of life in society.

That attitude is fundamentally corrosive because, if faith is not about the whole of life, it is not faith at all. What appears to be a gentle, reasonable form of secularism is in fact a denial of the very nature of religion. This is important to understand, because to go along with that proposition would undermine the very nature of faith. Faith is our response to God who *gives meaning to the whole of our lives and the whole of creation.* To put it more bluntly, insofar as a person views faith as a purely private matter unrelated to 'the real world', he or she is part of the advance of secularism.

We either believe with the whole of ourselves and with implications for the whole of our lives or we do not believe in God as God. To put it another way, a god who is relevant only to some parts of my life and only to some aspects of the world is not God at all. Bearing witness to our faith does not simply mean 'defending a space for God in our lives'; after all, our lives are entirely his! Faith means receiving and witnessing to God's word 'for what it really is, God's message and not some human thinking' (1 Thess 2:13).

Why is this important for understanding the role of the laity in the Church? The Church is the community of those who believe in God as God, as the source of all that exists. It is the community based on the call of God, the voice that speaks in our hearts: 'Their conscience is people's most secret core and their sanctuary. There they are alone with God whose voice echoes in their depths.'[14] The *Catechism of the Catholic Church* puts it eloquently:

---

14. *Gaudium et Spes*, 16.

The heart is the dwelling-place where I am, where I live; according to the Semitic or Biblical expression, the heart is the place 'to which I withdraw.' The heart is our hidden centre, beyond the grasp of our reason and of others; only the Spirit of God can fathom the human heart and know it fully. The heart is the place of decision, deeper than our psychic drives. It is the place of truth, where we choose life or death. It is the place of encounter, because as image of God we live in relation: it is the place of covenant.[15]

The word 'church', *ecclesia*, means those who are called out. That word is used to describe the people called forth by God into his Church. So the community gathered for the Eucharist is gathered by what is deepest within them, the voice of God whom we encounter in our hearts and whose call is a call to decision and truth and the choice between life and death. God calls each of us to be who he has invited us to be. We are gathered by the Holy Spirit who bears witness with our spirit that we are children of God (Rm 8:16).

A congregation sharing in the Eucharist is entirely different from the members of a sports club or an institution or a company attending their annual general meeting. Only a very sad human being *literally* lives for the mission statement or goals of his or her company or club or institution. They are one priority among many. Life is about more than one's work or one's sports club. These are the kind of involvements about which one can appropriately say that they should keep a certain sense of proportion – we speak of the importance of maintaining a 'work-life balance'. These involvements, however absorbing and however much they give rise to moments of intense commitment, are not the whole of life.

Belonging to an institution may be very important to people and may give rise to intense feelings of loyalty and involvement,

---

15. *Catechism of the Catholic Church*, 2563.

but is an involvement which is partial and limited. Belonging to a community in the fullest sense of the word is a deeper reality. Family and faith, for instance, are things that we don't put away into a box when we are not directly involved with them. They influence everything we do. We do not feel it is exaggerated or inappropriate when a person says, 'I live for my family'. We belong to our families with the whole of who we are. A family, ideally, is a place where people relate to one another with the whole of themselves.

Even that bond can be broken. Sad though it may be, people can and do walk away and live apparently fulfilled lives without any apparent connection with or loyalty to their family.

Our gathering in response to the voice of God is more than the bond of a human family. God is the goal and meaning of our whole lives, of the lives of all those we love, and of every human life. The voice of God is the voice which called us into existence and which calls us in his Incarnate Word, who is our Way, our Truth and our Life. If we are not open to that voice, we are not open to who we are. The person who has lost sight of God cannot see him/herself in the way that Blessed John Paul described in his first encyclical. There he said that in order to understand ourselves fully, we have to enter into ourselves and see ourselves in the light of the Incarnation and Redemption:

> If this intimate process takes place within a human being, it bears the fruit not only of adoration of God but also of deep wonder at oneself … In fact, that deep amazement at human worth and dignity is called the Gospel, in other words: the Good News. It is also called Christianity.[16]

It is perhaps more than a coincidence that in his last encyclical, Pope John Paul returned to the idea of 'deep amazement' but

---

16. JOHN PAUL II, *Redemptor Hominis*, 10.

this time in relation to the Eucharist. He wrote of how in the institution of the Eucharist the whole of the paschal mystery is gathered up, and he went on: 'The thought of this leads us to profound amazement and gratitude', adding, 'I would like to rekindle this Eucharistic "amazement" by the present Encyclical Letter.'[17]

This wonder and amazement leads to a sense of mission:

> The Church's fundamental function in every age and particularly in our own is to direct people's gaze, to point the awareness and experience of the whole of humanity towards the mystery of God, to help all people to be familiar with the profundity of the Redemption taking place in Christ Jesus. At the same time the deepest sphere of the person is involved – we mean the sphere of the human heart, conscience and life.[18]

THE SUMMIT AND THE SOURCE

Whether he did it consciously or not, Pope John Paul's echoing of the word 'amazement' in reference to the dignity of the human person in his first encyclical and in relation to the Eucharist in his last, says something very important. Reflecting on the role of the Christian and particularly the lay Christian in the world leads directly into a reflection on the meaning of the Eucharist as the central act of the liturgy, 'the summit toward which the activity of the Church is directed; at the same time it is the font from which all her power flows'.[19]

But what exactly is the relationship between the Eucharist and our daily lives? Pope Benedict spoke of the call of Vatican II for more active participation by the congregation in the celebration of Mass, and its statement that lay people are not meant to be

17. JOHN PAUL II, *Ecclesia de Eucharistia*, 5, 6.
18. *Redemptor Hominis*, 10.
19. VATICAN II, *Sacrosanctum Concilium*, 10.

simply silent spectators.[20] He pointed out that this is not just a matter of external activity, like singing hymns, doing readings and bidding prayers, offertory processions and so on – all of which are important. Much more fundamentally, it means 'greater awareness of the mystery being celebrated *and its relationship to daily life*', and he says, quoting Vatican II, that 'the faithful ... should give thanks to God. Offering the immaculate Victim, not only through the hands of the priest but also together with him, *they should learn to make an offering of themselves.*'[21]

St Augustine says that when the priest offers someone the Host, saying 'the Body of Christ', and the person replies 'Amen', he or she is not only saying 'Yes, I believe this is the Body of Christ' but is also saying, 'Yes, I believe that we are the Body of Christ'. Augustine says, 'You are saying yes to your own mystery',[22] or to put it in other words, you are saying yes to who you are. He quotes St Paul: 'You are the body of Christ and individually members of it' (1 Cor 12:27). And he says to his listeners: 'Be a member of Christ's body, then, so that your "Amen" may ring true!'[23]

What is offered to God in the Mass is the sacrifice of Christ on Calvary, made present for us. The sacrifice of Christ is not only the sacrifice of his life, it is the sacrifice of all those who, as St Paul put it, share in his sufferings so as to become like him in his death (Phil 3:10). Writing to the Colossians, he said: 'Now I rejoice in my sufferings for your sake, and in my flesh I complete what is lacking in Christ's afflictions for the sake of his body that is the church' (Col 1:24).

His afflictions are over. Christ, the Head of the Body, is in the eternal glory he had with his Father before the creation (Jn 17:5). But his Body, which we are, is still on the road, still passing through the sufferings through which he became the first born

---

20. Ibid., 48.
21. BENEDICT XVI, *Sacramentum Caritatis*, 52; *Sacrosanctum Concilium*, 49 (my italics).
22. *Sermon 272*.
23. AUGUSTINE, *Sermon 272*.

from the dead, and through whom the Father reconciled all things to himself (Col 1:15-20).

We are members of his body (Eph 5:30). In the Eucharist we recognise that what we suffer is united to what he suffered. Our suffering is the suffering of the Body of Christ which we are. The role of everyone who is present at Mass is to offer him or herself along with the self-offering of Jesus on the Cross. So everyone in the Church is offering to God the sacrifice of Christ and at the same time and inseparably each one is offering his or her own life and every aspect of it. And so we are all sharers in the priesthood of Christ, what is called 'the universal priesthood' or 'the priesthood of all the faithful'.

The Second Vatican Council puts it like this:

> To [the laity] whom he intimately joins to his life and mission, [Christ] also gives a share in his priestly office of offering spiritual worship for the glory of the Father and the salvation of humanity. Hence the laity, dedicated as they are to Christ and anointed by the Holy Spirit, are marvellously called and prepared so that ever richer fruits of the Spirit may be produced in them. For all their works, if accomplished in the Spirit, become 'spiritual sacrifices acceptable to God through Jesus Christ': their prayers and apostolic undertakings, family and married life, their daily work, relaxation of mind and body, even the hardships of life, if patiently born (cf. 1 Pt 2:5). In the celebration of the Eucharist, these are offered to the Father in all piety along with the body of the Lord. And so, worshipping everywhere by their holy actions, *the laity consecrate the world itself to God*.[24]

This is true for everyone who takes part in the celebration, including the priest. Priests too are baptised Christians, part of

---

24. VATICAN II, *Lumen Gentium*, 34 (my italics).

the priesthood of all the faithful. With all the participants, the priest also offers his life, and hopes and fears, his relationship with the people of the parish community, with friends and family, his anxieties and his thankfulness. All of us offer to the Father our activities and achievements – what Vatican II called 'all the good fruits of our nature and enterprise'[25] – to be received as part of the Body of Christ into the new creation.

This is the summit and the source of the life of every Christian because this is the fundamental meaning of all that we do and are. The way to the new creation is through the Paschal Mystery. Christ is the first born. His human nature, his body in which he became a member of the human family, has already entered the glory that is our hope. We believe that all humanity is called to that glory in him.

So at Mass we unite everything in our lives and in our world to that passage which Jesus Christ has already made. We believe that we will find again the fruits of our nature and enterprise, human dignity, solidarity, freedom – freed from sin, freed from impermanence and imperfection – when Christ presents to his Father an eternal and universal kingdom 'of truth and life, a kingdom of holiness and grace, a kingdom of justice, love and peace'.[26]

God has called all of us to be priests: 'You are a chosen race, a royal priesthood, a holy nation, God's own people, in order that you may proclaim the mighty acts of him who called you out of darkness into his marvellous light' (1 Pt 2:9).

We come as priests to make the offering of our own lives. We offer all our efforts to bring the Gospel to the new continent, we offer the lives of our families, the lives of our neighbours, the hopes and fears, the achievements and failures, and we say: 'This is where all of these things and events find their meaning;

---

25. See *Gaudium et Spes*, 39.
26. *Gaudium et Spes*, 39.

this is where everybody, those close to me and the whole human family finds hope.' And this offering becomes part of the human family's unique role as the only part of creation that can freely and consciously praise its Creator. The priesthood of all the baptised is not just a part of that role but the highest point of it:

> Through the human person, spokesperson for all creation, all living things praise the Lord. Our breath of life that also presupposes self-knowledge, awareness, and freedom becomes the song and prayer of the whole of life that vibrates in the universe.[27]

This is in no sense to play down the ordained or ministerial priesthood. It is only the presence of the ordained priest that makes this an assembly of those called to celebrate in union with the bishop, and in union with the Church throughout the world, as an act of Christ our Head. A congregation gathered for the Eucharist is not just a group of people who happen to have come together, but an *ecclesia*, a congregation gathered by the call of Christ which is also the call of the Church. That is what is made visible by the presence of the priest in the person of Christ the Head, the One who calls. The priest not only calls the congregation together, he also acts in the name and in the person of Christ the Head when he speaks the Eucharistic Prayer which recalls and makes present Christ's offering of himself at the Last Supper and in the agony of Calvary and his entry into glory.

But neither should we play down the universal priesthood – the two kinds of priesthood belong together:

> While the common priesthood of the faithful is exercised by the unfolding of baptismal grace – a life of faith, hope, and charity, a life according to the Spirit – the ministerial

---

27. JOHN PAUL II, General Audience, 9 January 2002.

priesthood is at the service of the common priesthood. It is directed at the unfolding of the baptismal grace of all Christians. The ministerial priesthood is a means by which Christ unceasingly builds up and leads his Church.[28]

EUCHARISTIC IN OUR DAY

It is particularly important in our day to see this offering of ourselves and our lives in the light of the fundamental reality of the offering of Christ and his suffering. We are living at a time where, for all our readiness to complain, we are in fact not well able to deal with suffering. It is within, or almost within, living memory that infant and child mortality was common in Ireland. Many killer diseases of the early twentieth century are not life-threatening anymore. There is a strong tendency, when suffering hits us, even if no one is at fault, to feel that this should not have happened and that somebody must be accountable. We are disturbed when we encounter cases where medicine is powerless to help.

But although the material pain of disease and hunger and illness are less acute than they were for past generations, in other ways we may be poorer. We can be cut off from our roots; we can be isolated from ourselves. As someone put it, it is very lonely when you don't know anybody – even yourself. It is a world which doesn't like silence, and which leaves little space for deep reflection. People now spend their whole waking lives attached to an iPod or the radio. We go to a social occasion, like a wedding or a Christmas party, and the music is so loud that communication is impossible. There may be a doctoral thesis to be written about a society that thinks that social occasions should be organised in such a way as to make it as difficult as possible for the people who are present to communicate with one another.

We are also living in a world where it is harder to believe and it is harder to live one's faith without embarrassment. It is a world where we know we are seen by many of our contemporaries as

28. *Catechism of the Catholic Church*, 1547.

people caught up in an outdated and irrational understanding of life.

Many people are disheartened today because so much that seemed to be good in Irish Catholicism has been tarnished or has diminished. We need to be more humble – but not humiliated or silenced. We need to be clear that our strength is not in our own achievements. We follow Christ who died in agony, who suffered abandonment, betrayal, injustice and mockery. When we look back at a time when our churches were full, our seminaries bursting at the seams, our missionaries all over the world, we may wonder whether in those 'good old days' we might have succumbed to the temptation to pray like the Pharisee, thanking God that we are not like other people (cf. Lk 18:11). When everything seems to be going well, followers of Christ should understand that complacency is never the authentic tone of Christian living!

When we find ourselves in the pain of Good Friday or in the emptiness of Holy Saturday, then we are more likely to be on the Way he showed us than when we are feeling smug and satisfied. Our belonging does not consist in sitting prematurely on thrones at his right and left, but in following together with him and in union with one another along the often painful way on which he leads us. Do we really believe in our hearts what St Paul said, 'When I am weak, then I am strong' (2 Cor 12:10)?

The Passion of Jesus is an account of absolute horror – a man abandoned by his friends, sweating blood at the prospect he faced, unjustly condemned at the behest of a mob demanding his death, a man scourged and mocked, dying in helpless, shameful agony hanging on a cross. It was a punishment so terrible that even the thought of treating a Roman citizen in such a way was viewed with complete revulsion. Crucifixion was a cruel penalty that could be inflicted only on a slave or a foreigner. Cicero, in the course of making an indignant and horrified indictment of a man called Gaius Verres responsible for having crucified a Roman citizen, called it 'the most extreme and ultimate punishment fit only for slaves'. Even a writer so renowned for his eloquence was lost for words. The horror of crucifying a Roman citizen, he said, 'cannot by any possibility be adequately expressed by any name bad enough for it'.[29]

The culture we are living in in the western world, and indeed in Ireland, may well become increasingly intolerant of religion. We need to draw strength from the realisation that our faith is *founded* on the worst that can happen. The death and resurrection of Christ, which is the core of the Eucharistic celebration, is the most eloquent possible demonstration that the love of God is stronger than any disaster or loss.

The French writer Georges Bernanos imagines a scene where a courageous, or perhaps foolhardy, parish priest invites the local agnostic to address the congregation. The agnostic says that, although he doesn't believe, he occasionally looks at believers with the faint hope that they might be right. His challenge went something like this: 'You say you believe that the infinite God loves each one of you so much that he sent his eternal Son to die for you. You believe that you will share the infinite life and love of God forever. How amazing that would be if it were true! You believe that when you receive absolution you are in what you call "the state of grace".' And he goes on:

> 'The state of grace.' Well, what more do you want? It doesn't seem to mean very much to you. We ask ourselves, what do you do with the grace of God? Where the devil do you hide your joy? Surely it should be shining out of you![30]

When one looks at the Church in Ireland today, the question arises, 'Where do you hide your joy?'; 'where is the fire that should

---

29. In Verr., II.V. 66: '*servitutis extremum summumque supplicium*'.
30. BERNANOS, G., *Les Grandes cimetières sous la lune*, Paris: Plon, 1938, p. 310 (my translation).

be burning?' A great variety of lay movements, from the Legion of Mary to YCW to *Comunione e Liberazione*, have enkindled the fire of vibrant living. Rather than simply lamenting the lack of enthusiasm we see around us, we should look to places where *the enthusiasm actually exists* and try to learn something.

Clearly not every movement will suit every individual or every parish; clearly too, movements need to examine themselves regularly on how they relate to the wider Christian community and acknowledge the risk of developing an attitude that sees themselves as a kind of elite. Everyone needs to be aware of the risk of coming to believe that 'I am not as the rest of men'. But we need to recognise the great value and indeed the necessity of groupings in which people can share their joy and express their Christian commitment in their lives. The most risky policy of all is to imagine that without a real, serious effort of renewal, things will somehow work out.

The Eucharist is not just the summit of the Christian life but also its source. The universal priesthood is not just about offering oneself and one's life to God, it is about recognising that really hearing God's invitation, really thanking and worshipping the God who calls us, cannot stop there. It demands of us that we speak that call to others, that we do not hide our joy:

> [The laity] are consecrated for the royal priesthood and the holy people (cf. 1 Pt 2:4-10) not only that they may offer spiritual sacrifices in everything they do but also that they may witness to Christ throughout the world.[31]

One of the changes made in the Missal at the specific request of Pope Benedict and indeed Pope John Paul, was that the forms of sending out the congregation at the end of Mass should be made more effective. Some new formulas have been provided, which

---

31. *Apostolicam Actuositatem*, 3.

send the congregation out on a mission: 'Go and announce the Gospel of the Lord'; 'Go in peace, glorifying the Lord by your life.'

We need to grasp the truth of the priesthood of all believers, clearly restated by the Second Vatican Council. We are the people who are meant to live and to celebrate the very meaning of life – '[God's] plan for the fullness of time, to gather up all things in [Christ], things in heaven and things on earth' (Eph 1:10).

✺

CHAPTER FOUR

The Mystery of Humanity

VATICAN II TOOK PLACE during what became known as 'the Swinging Sixties'. It was a time of optimism and hope. One of the most significant documents of the Council was called 'Joy and Hope' *(Gaudium et Spes)*. It did indeed reflect something, perhaps too much, of that atmosphere of optimism. The 1960s had a less positive side: they were marked by the widespread use of drugs, by promiscuity and war. The first sentence of the document, from which it took its title, was not unrealistic about the negative side of life:

> The joys and the hopes, the grief and the anguish of the people of our time, especially of those who are poor or afflicted are the joys and the hopes, the grief and anguish of the followers of Christ as well.[1]

The Council had considered the Church in many dimensions of its life: God's revelation, the liturgy, education, ecumenism etc. This document, published at the end of the final session, turned to the wider world, to the whole of humanity. It reflected a particular concern of the Council:

> Never before perhaps, so much as on this occasion, has the Church felt the need to know, to draw near to, to understand, to penetrate, serve and evangelise the society in which she lives; and to get to grips with it, almost to run after it, in its rapid and continuous change.[2]

---

1.   VATICAN II, *Gaudium et Spes,* Pastoral Constitution on the Church in the Modern World, 1.
2.   PAUL VI, Address at the last General Meeting of the Second Vatican Council, 7 December 1965.

Gaudium et Spes is designated as a '*Pastoral* Constitution'.[3] It addresses issues such as the family, culture, war and peace. These are matters that are seriously affected by the 'rapid and continuous change' in society. Fifty years later, the world is enormously different. Many of these changing issues have been addressed in the intervening years in the social encyclicals, in the *Compendium of the Social Doctrine of the Church* and in many documents of episcopal conferences, of individual bishops, in the work of theologians and in the work of many Christians involved in the life of society.

Bishop Karol Wojtyła, later Pope John Paul II, played a significant part in drafting *Gaudium et Spes*, and his later teaching and encyclicals are in many respects an expansion and commentary on the Pastoral Constitution.

KNOW THYSELF[4]

The earlier part of *Gaudium et Spes* deals with matters which are primarily theological and philosophical – and in the first place with the question, 'what is a human being?' A reflection on that question forms the basis for understanding the activity of the Church and of Christians in the world. The question of the meaning of human life has been fundamental throughout history as Pope John Paul pointed out in his encyclical *Fides et Ratio*:

> … in different parts of the world, with their different cultures, there arise at the same time the fundamental questions which pervade human life: *Who am I? Where have I come from and where am I going? Why is there evil? What is there after this life?* These are the questions which we find in the sacred writings

---

3. There are three other constitutions among the documents of Vatican II. These four documents are described as 'the true pillars of the Council' (see Note with Pastoral Recommendations for the Year of Faith, CDF, 2012). The designation 'Pastoral Constitution' is unique.

4. The ancient Greek phrase, transliterated as *gnothi seauton*, is attributed to various sages.

of Israel, as also in the Veda and the Avesta; we find them in
the writings of Confucius and Lao Tze, and in the preaching
of Tirthankara and Buddha; they appear in the poetry of
Homer and in the tragedies of Euripides and Sophocles, as
they do in the philosophical writings of Plato and Aristotle.
They are questions which have their common source in the
quest for meaning which has always compelled the human
heart. In fact, the answer given to these questions decides the
direction which people seek to give to their lives.[5]

The introduction of the encyclical is headed 'Know Yourself'.
That advice, formulated in ancient Greece, underlies the whole
human quest for knowledge. The human being is characterised
precisely by being 'oriented towards knowing him/herself'.[6]
Learning to understand our own potential and limitations, our
biases and partial perspectives is important to try to ensure that
they do not distort what we think we know. We see things very
differently according to our circumstances, our mood, or the
attitude of people around us. It is said that we don't see things
as they are; we see them as we are. Our own longings, and in
particular our search for truth, drive the entire quest.

The book *Bad Science* has a chapter which asks, 'Why do
clever people believe stupid things?'[7] The author points out
that one reason why errors occur is that so many factors tend to
distort our perception, such as social influences, our tendency
to give more emphasis to something because it seems unusual
or striking, or the temptation to seek the solution that suits us.
We often approach a problem with an assumption that we know
the answer; we can sometimes find a pattern where none exists.

5.   JOHN PAUL II, *Fides et Ratio*, On the Relationship of Faith and Reason, 1; see
Gaudium et Spes, 10.
6.   PONTIFICAL COUNCIL FOR JUSTICE AND PEACE, *Compendium of the
Social Teaching of the Church*, 14.
7.   GOLDACRE, B., *Bad Science*, London: Fourth Estate, 2009.

When we form a hypothesis, we are inclined to look for evidence to confirm it rather than evidence which might refute it: 'It seems that we have an innate tendency to seek out and overvalue evidence that confirms a given hypothesis.'[8]

Failure to understand ourselves, our strengths and our limitations, and especially failure to understand the kind of beings we are, may mean that what we imagine to be objective conclusions have been distorted by presuppositions and interpretations which we wrongly imagine to be self-evident.

In recent centuries we have learned how important it is to look at the world through a scientific lens. We have come to imagine that this is an entirely objective and unbiased way to examine realities. But scientists are well aware that in the very act of making an observation, we are already interpreting and even changing what we are analysing. Most strikingly, at the level of quantum mechanics, our normal way of measuring and perceiving reality is entirely misleading:

> [Hiesenberg's paper in 1927] showed that not only the determinism of classical physics must be abandoned, but also the naive concept of reality which looked upon the particles of atomic physics as if they were very small grains of sand. At every instant a grain of sand has a definite position and velocity. This is not the case with an electron. If its position is determined with increasing accuracy, the possibility of ascertaining the velocity becomes less and *vice versa*.[9]

Even more seriously, there is a danger in our time that the scientific method, because it has produced such dramatic and abundant results, might come to be seen as the only valid kind of knowledge.

---

8. *Bad Science*, p. 247.

9. BORN, M, 'The statistical interpretation of quantum mechanics', Nobel Lecture, 11 December 1954. http://www.nobelprize.org/nobel_prizes/physics/laureates/1954/born-lecture.pdf.

There are forms of knowledge which are not the product of laboratory experiments or mathematical reasoning. There is the kind of knowledge that is called 'wisdom'. That can be expressed in poetry and religion, in music and literature, in human relationships and reflectiveness, in the ability to see beyond the superficial and the immediate, and in a particular way in religious faith.

Without wisdom, what will direct and evaluate the progress of science and technology?[10] The idea that nothing can be considered true unless it can be established by the scientific method would be a great truncation of the range of human knowledge. When that happens, instead of broadening our horizons, an exclusive concentration on science, by undervaluing wisdom, may actually narrow them. When that happens:

> … only the kind of certainty resulting from the interplay of mathematical and empirical elements can be considered scientific. Anything that would claim to be science must be measured against this criterion. Hence the human sciences, such as history, psychology, sociology and philosophy, attempt to conform themselves to this canon [of what constitutes science].[11] A second point, which is important for our reflections, is that by its very nature this method excludes the question of God, making it appear an unscientific or pre-scientific question. Consequently, we are faced with a reduction of the radius of science and reason, one which needs to be questioned.[12]

The observation of *Gaudium et Spes* is as apt as it was when it was written:

---

10. See *Gaudium et Spes*, 15.
11. The official translation rather inelegantly says 'canon of scientificity'.
12. BENEDICT XVI, Address at the University of Regensburg, 12 September 2006.

Our age, more than any of the past, needs such wisdom if all humanity's discoveries are to be ennobled through human effort. Indeed the future of the world is in danger unless wiser people are forthcoming.[13]

WHO AM I?

Blessed John Paul II pointed to a much deeper reason as to why the question 'Who am I?' is so central:

> [The human being] must, so to speak, enter into [Christ] with all his own self, he must 'appropriate' and assimilate the whole of the reality of the Incarnation and Redemption in order to find himself. If this profound process takes place within him, he then bears fruit not only of adoration of God but also of deep wonder at himself ... In reality, the name for that deep amazement at man's worth and dignity is the Gospel, that is to say: the Good News. It is also called Christianity.[14]

This is the heart of the challenge that Pope John Paul, reflecting on Vatican II, put to the Church at the beginning of his pontificate.

What would our parish councils, our congregations, our dioceses, indeed our whole world, look like if we understood the Good News in those terms? What would be the effect on us and on the world if, after profound reflection on ourselves in the light of Christ, we really were filled with deep wonder and amazement at the worth and dignity of ourselves and of every human being?

In the early part of *Gaudium et Spes*, we find one of the passages from the Council documents which Pope John Paul cited more frequently than any of the others. It indicates that the human person cannot fully understand him/herself simply through

---

13. *Gaudium et Spes*, 15.
14. JOHN PAUL II, *Redemptor Hominis*, 10.

scientific research. Full understanding requires the perspective of religion and in particular of the revelation in Christ; it also involves the kind of life which reflects the reality of God who is love:

> In reality it is only in the mystery of the Word made flesh that the mystery of humanity truly becomes clear. For Adam, the first man, was a type of him who was to come, Christ the Lord. Christ, the new Adam, in the very revelation of the mystery of the Father and his love, fully reveals humanity to itself and brings to light its very high calling.[15]

Discussion of the question 'who am I?' is not just theoretical; it could not be more practical and contemporary. An adequate answer is crucial in looking at all the great issues. No matter how much information about ourselves may be obtained by the scientific method, it will not answer the question in all of its dimensions. Most especially, it will not answer the fundamental question about the meaning of human life:

> It is man himself who ends up being reduced, for the specifically human questions about our origin and destiny, the questions raised by religion and ethics, then have no place within the purview of collective reason as defined by 'science' and must thus be relegated to the realm of the subjective.[16]

The temptation is to imagine that science and its technological fruits could explain everything in the world. Human beings are not just particularly complicated machines. The physics and biology of human life are indeed complex, but they do not exhaust the reality of human experience. No machine could produce an

---

15. *Gaudium et Spes*, 22.
16. Address at the University of Regensburg.

artistic masterpiece except by accident, and even then it would have no idea that it was a masterpiece or why.

Of course, mathematical patterns of great complexity and beauty can be produced by a computer. No matter how remarkably a machine might reproduce and combine the best qualities of the works of great artists, the result would lack the essence of genuine art. That has to do with human longings and the unbridgeable gap between our longings and our present reality, it has to do with birth and death, loss and hope, joy and grief, the search for meaning and truth and beauty.

This personal search and longing opens a path into a deeper knowledge of ourselves and the meaning of our lives. Speaking at Christmas Midnight Mass in 2011, Pope Benedict said:

> It seems to me that a deeper truth is revealed here, which should touch our hearts on this holy night: if we want to find the God who appeared as a child, then we must dismount from the high horse of our 'enlightened' reason. We must set aside our false certainties, our intellectual pride, which prevents us from recognising God's closeness. We must follow the interior path of Saint Francis – the path leading to that ultimate outward and inward simplicity which enables the heart to see. We must bend down, spiritually we must as it were go on foot, in order to pass through the portal of faith and encounter the God who is so different from our prejudices and opinions – the God who conceals himself in the humility of a newborn baby.[17]

SEARCHING FOR TRUTH AND BEAUTY

That quest for truth is at the heart of human existence: 'One may define the human being, therefore, as *the one who seeks the*

---

17. BENEDICT XVI, Homily, 24 December 2011.

truth.'[18] Science is an important part of the human search for the truth. But the whole search for truth is related also to the quest for goodness, unity and beauty.

This is often evident in the work of scientists. The solution to a scientific investigation may be elegant and even beautiful. Indeed, it may be that the elegance of a possible solution is what, consciously or unconsciously, prompts the scientist to test it and demonstrate it.

Beauty and goodness and unity are listed, along with truth, as what traditional philosophy called the transcendentals. These are all concepts which contain no intrinsic limitation within them. In this they differ from a quality like colour. There is a limit to how dark a shade of blue or red or green can become, because in the end it becomes black, or how light it can become because eventually it becomes white. In other words, if you push it far enough, it ceases to be blue or red or green. But there is no intrinsic limit to goodness or beauty or truth or unity; they exist without any limit in God.

Similarly there can be no such thing as the highest possible number or the heaviest possible weight. Such qualities as amounts and weights cannot be attributed to God because they cannot exist in an infinite form. This is nicely illustrated by the story of the little girl who asked her mother what was the highest number. The mother gently explained that there could be no such thing. No matter how many gazillion trillion you produced, all someone had to say was 'and one' to produce a higher number. After a while, the little girl said, 'Now I know the answer – the highest possible number is God'. She was obviously something of a theologian. She had understood that God is not the kind of being which can be made greater by adding 'and one'. God is not the kind of being which can be subjected to any experiment, or measured by any instrument, however sophisticated.

---

18. *Fides et Ratio,* 28 (italics in original).

The beauty which can be attributed to God – in a form more perfect than we can even imagine – must also be true and good. It therefore carries within it a longing for the absolute, unlimited, undying beauty, goodness and truth which we do not find in our experience on earth. That is why no scientific method can exhaust the essence of what it means to be human. We start out on the quest for unlimited beauty, truth and goodness because there is something within us that prompts the search:

> It is unthinkable that a search so deeply rooted in human nature would be completely vain and useless. The capacity to search for truth and to pose questions itself implies the rudiments of a response. Human beings would not even begin to search for something of which they knew nothing or for something which they thought was wholly beyond them. Only the sense that they can arrive at an answer leads them to take the first step.[19]

In his first encyclical, *Redemptor Hominis*, Pope John Paul described the 'creative restlessness' in which we find what is most deeply human: 'the search for truth, the insatiable need for the good … nostalgia for the beautiful'.[20]

The tension, the restlessness which underlies artistic creativity arises precisely from the fact that we are incapable of providing for ourselves anything that would completely and permanently satisfy that search. Still less can we provide it for every one of our brothers and sisters. Whatever sense we could create for ourselves is necessarily incomplete because it could not be shared by the whole human race. Even if I could totally satisfy my own longings, there is no reason to imagine that everybody else would be happy in my utopia! One small bubble of abundant meaning,

---

19. Ibid., 29.
20. *Redemptor Hominis*, 18.

even if an inconceivably fortunate individual could enjoy it, would remain absurd if it were not part of a world big enough to make sense of human life for all. We need all those smaller moments of happiness, achievement and peace, but they serve only to intensify the quest.

> ... anyone who does not know God, even though he may entertain all kinds of hopes, is ultimately without hope, without the great hope that sustains the whole of life (cf. Eph 2:12). Man's great, true hope which holds firm in spite of all disappointments can only be God – God who has loved us and who continues to love us 'to the end,' until all 'is accomplished' (cf. Jn 13:1 and 19:30).[21]

Nothing that can be measured can satisfy the longings of the human heart. The use of the word 'nostalgia' in connection with our longing for the beautiful is very evocative. The beauty of nature or of art touches longings which this world can never satisfy. G. K. Chesterton challenged those who put forward rationalistic arguments to discredit Christian faith: 'Give me an explanation ... of the vast human tradition of some ancient happiness ...'[22] Christianity, he said, allowed people not just to look back towards a paradise lost forever, but to look forward to a fulfilment that makes sense of those longings.

The nostalgia for that ancient happiness, or the 'great true hope', can keep our horizons open and prevent us from becoming trapped in too narrow a view of truth and of ourselves. While it may not have been what he meant, the question attributed to Dostoevsky may point to a profound truth: 'Will beauty save the world?'

---

21. BENEDICT XVI, *Spe Salvi*, 27.
22. CHESTERTON, G. K., *Orthodoxy*, http://www.gutenberg.org/files/16769/16769-h/16769-h.htm; accessed 6 March 2012.

And so perhaps that old trinity of Truth and Good and Beauty is not just the formal outworn formula it used to seem to us during our heady, materialistic youth. If the crests of these three trees join together, as the investigators and explorers used to affirm, and if the too obvious, too straight branches of Truth and Good are crushed or amputated and cannot reach the light – yet perhaps the whimsical, unpredictable, unexpected branches of Beauty will make their way through and soar up to that very place and in this way perform the work of all three. And in that case it was not a slip of the tongue for Dostoevsky to say that 'Beauty will save the world,' but a prophecy. After all, he was given the gift of seeing much, he was extraordinarily illumined.[23]

The light shines most brightly in the darkness, but it is also true that for many people the darkness seems impenetrable. The experience of darkness is particularly characteristic of the world of our time, which has seen so many tragedies and wars. As Pope John Paul put it, 'Our age speaks of the silence or absence of God.'[24] The eloquent silence of God speaks a word that is large enough to bring fulfilment to people of every race, language, culture and time:

> For true justice must include everyone; it must bring the answer to the immense load of suffering borne by all the generations. In fact, without the resurrection of the dead and the Lord's judgement, there is no justice in the full sense of the term.[25]

---

23. SOLZHENITSYN, Aleksandr, *Beauty Will Save the World,* http://www.mro.org/mr/archive/24-2/articles/beauty.html; accessed 6 March 2012.
24. JOHN PAUL II, *Master in the Faith* (1990), 14, 15, 16.
25. CONGREGATION FOR THE DOCTRINE OF THE FAITH, Instruction on Christian Freedom and Liberation, 60.

WHO ARE WE?

One cannot reflect on the question 'who am I?' without at the same time asking 'who are we?' That is particularly evident when we look to the unknown future which we have to share on this vulnerable planet, afflicted by so many injustices and dangers. The second of the two passages of Vatican II most frequently quoted by Pope John Paul says:

> [T]he Lord Jesus, when praying to his Father, 'that they may all be one … even as we are one' (Jn 17:21-22) has opened up new horizons closed to human reason by indicating that there is a certain similarity between the union existing among the divine persons and the union of God's children in truth and love. It follows then that, if human beings are the only creatures on earth that God has wanted for their own sake, they can fully discover their true selves only in sincere self-giving.[26]

By the middle of this century humanity will be sharing a very different world. The twenty-first century may see new kinds of darkness: wars about basic resources, the escalating effects of climate change, political instability and new forms of terrorism. The world by mid-century may well have seen the end of the economic, political and cultural dominance of what we call 'the West'. In the Church, the great majority of Catholics will live in Latin America, Africa and Asia and the proportion of Europeans will have diminished.

This century may also see enormous advances in science, technology, especially nanotechnology, medical research and communications that we cannot even imagine. Those who today are at the cutting edge of new technology will probably feel like dinosaurs. Like all advances, these will need to be guided by a wise appreciation of who we are.

---

26. *Gaudium et Spes*, 24.

It is clear that in Ireland and elsewhere, society badly needs a vision that is capable of uniting us as a community with a common goal. This cannot be simply about political and economic programmes. It will have to face the deeper issues to which the Council pointed. As we face a world in extraordinarily rapid change, we cannot ignore the fundamental questions: 'Who am I? Where have I come from and where am I going? Why is there evil? What is there after this life?' That is not to say that everybody has to agree on the answers. Nevertheless, a society which is aware that these are the vital human questions would at least have a basis for a real dialogue. To understand and recognise the importance of beliefs and convictions about the meaning of human life is the foundation of tolerance. Tolerance is not indifference; it means appreciating and trying to understand the place that the beliefs of other people and groups have in their lives.

Without some understanding of the centrality of these issues, it is difficult to envisage any coherent or adequate vision of where we want to go as a society. If the future is to be civilised in any proper sense, its members will have to relate to one another with a respect for their real dignity and an understanding of how important the questions of meaning are. Dialogue between people only reaches its true significance 'on the deeper level of interpersonal relationships. These demand a mutual respect for the full spiritual dignity of the person.'[27] They demand sincere mutual gift of ourselves to one another.

THE LOVE OF GOD MADE VISIBLE
Self-giving is how human beings find themselves; it is the meaning of human relationships. That is because of a more fundamental truth. Human self-giving reflects the mutual self-giving of the

----
27. Ibid., 23.

divine life itself. We human beings are at our best when we sincerely give ourselves to others, because we are created in the image and likeness of a self-giving God. In our relationships with each other the love of God is made visible. That is what it means to be Church, 'a sacrament or as a sign and instrument both of a very closely knit union with God and of the unity of the whole human race':

> [The Word made flesh] revealed to us that 'God is love' (1 Jn 4:8) and at the same time taught us that the new command of love was the basic law of human perfection and hence of the world's transformation.[28]

This forms the basis for the Council's treatment of the particular issues it addresses in society. In the family, the love of God supports husband and wife 'in order that by their mutual self-giving spouses will love each other with enduring fidelity'.[29] In economic activity Christians need the relevant skills and experience like any other person, but in addition they will try to ensure that 'their lives, individual as well as social, may be inspired by the spirit of the Beatitudes, and in particular by the spirit of poverty'.[30] Although the political arena has its own autonomy, when people engage in politics they do not leave their beliefs behind, 'For humanity's horizons are not confined to the temporal order; living in human history, they retain the fullness of their eternal calling.'[31] The search for peace in the world has to look to a kind of relationship which is not just the absence of violence or even the respecting of rights because, 'peace is … the fruit of love, for love goes beyond what justice can provide'.[32]

28. Ibid., 38.
29. Ibid., 49.
30. Ibid., 72.
31. Ibid., 76.
32. Ibid., 78.

But there is a more fundamental truth. In everything we have and are, we are receivers of God's gift. Even when a believer approaches another person, filled with the wonder and amazement of the Christian Gospel, he or she is bringing them awareness of a gift they have already been offered when the Creator spoke a creative and inviting word to them in the first moment of their existence; to put it another way, we can only bring them the knowledge of who they already are in the light of that invitation.[33]

Although Christians can and should be bearers of God's invitation to their brothers and sisters, that invitation always comes from God, not simply from a human being. The first moment of each human person's existence involves him or her being addressed and invited by God into a relationship. *Gaudium et Spes* says that 'The invitation to converse with God is addressed to men and women as soon as they come into being.'[34] Personhood cannot, therefore, be understood in individualistic terms. Every person is, from the beginning, in relationship to God and to other people.

'THE ASTONISHING EXPERIENCE OF GIFT'[35]

The understanding of the human person and human society which Pope John Paul elaborated using his two favourite passages from Vatican II reached fuller expression in the encyclicals of his successor. This is particularly the case in the truly remarkable Chapter 3 of the encyclical *Caritas in Veritate*. There Pope Benedict summed up his approach to life in society in what he called 'the principle of gratuitousness'.[36] The clumsiness of the English translation is in contrast to the profound simplicity of the concept. Everything that we have and are is totally gift. It follows

---

33. See Chapter 2, fn. 19.
34. *Gaudium et Spes*, 19. ('Ad colloquium cum Deo iam inde ab ortu suo invitatur homo.')
35. *Caritas in Veritate*, 34.
36. Ibid.

that nobody has any grounds for feeling superior to another. Terms like possessing and owning and entitlement do not apply in personal relationships. We do not own one another; we have no right to demand another's love or forgiveness; no human being is a mere instrument to be used but always an end in him or herself. God's way is different; it is about superabundant gift. The gift of God's love and hope 'bursts into our lives as something not due to us'.[37] It is a gift infinitely beyond our ability to achieve or to create. Unless we understand that, we are in no position to communicate it to anyone else.

In the life of Jesus, the different logic of superabundance goes beyond what could be demanded in terms of cold justice. In the Gospels, we see 'how Jesus moved beyond revenge, and beyond the Old Testament logic of equivalence (eye for an eye) to turn the other cheek and go the extra mile as in the Sermon on the Mount'.[38]

There is an overwhelming temptation to regard the statements of the Sermon on the Mount as hyperbole, not to be taken literally. It is, of course, true that it could never become a universal rule that a mugger who demands his victim's coat should be given his cloak as well. But is it something that the logic of superabundance might sometimes call for? Undoubtedly!

There can be no sense of gift without justice, but political and economic development 'if it is to be authentically human, needs to make room for the *principle of gratuitousness* as an expression of fraternity'.[39] Nor is this just an added dimension to justice:

> While in the past it was possible to argue that justice had to come first and gratuitousness could follow afterwards, as a

37. Ibid.
38. SCHINELLER, P., *Pope Benedict: A Call to a Higher Moral/Economic Plane*, *America* Magazine blog: 8 July 2009: http://www.americamagazine.org/blog/entry.cfm?blog_id=2&entry_id=2036.
39. *Caritas in Veritate*, 34.

complement, today it is clear that without gratuitousness, there can be no justice in the first place.[40]

Recent centuries have acquiesced in the assumption that politics and economics function according to their own rules, where the concept of gift is out of place and where it would be far too idealistic to try to import such 'woolly' ideas. What Pope Benedict is arguing is precisely that the harmony and unity that we seek to bring about in society is ultimately God's gift. The effort to create a more human society through ruthless competition, through violence, through coercion, is ultimately doomed. Community is built by charity-in-truth, 'a gift received by everyone'. When we are wrongly convinced that we are the sole authors of ourselves, our lives and our society, things becomes distorted and hope itself is destroyed:

> Then, the conviction that the economy must be autonomous, that it must be shielded from 'influences' of a moral character, has led man to abuse the economic process in a thoroughly destructive way. In the long term, these convictions have led to economic, social and political systems that trample upon personal and social freedom, and are therefore unable to deliver the justice that they promise.[41]

To put this in practical terms, when economic considerations become paramount, the welfare of individuals and of society, the common good, is no longer the goal of social activity. It is taken for granted that the main aim of company directors must be to maximise profits for their shareholders, whatever the effects on the workers, on the community or on the supply of scarce resources. Does the system require that directors must assume their shareholders to be amoral?

---

40. Ibid., 38.
41. Ibid., 34.

When Aer Lingus closed the Shannon-Heathrow route in 2007 – a decision that has since been reversed – the Bishops of the mid-west, Catholic and Church of Ireland, issued a statement which included the following points:

- ❧ We are particularly concerned that the Aer Lingus statement that this was a pragmatic commercial decision appears to be offered as a complete and adequate justification;

- ❧ The ultimate purpose of the economy and of economic activity is not just to create profit; it is to make life more human for people. There is no area of life, including the economy, in which social responsibility may be ignored. Nor do we accept that shareholders should be presumed to have no interest other than the generation of profit at whatever cost to their fellow human beings. That is especially true when the shareholder in the company is the government, which exists to foster the common good of its citizens;

- ❧ We cannot accept that managers and boards of companies may regard considerations such as the well-being of their staff, their obligations to their customers and their impact on the community and the wider world as matters of little relevance in serious decision making.[42]

Sometimes even people whose instincts are humane are driven into such decisions by the battle for survival in the 'real world' of cut-throat commerce. Pope John Paul had already indicated that the system itself is flawed:

It is obvious that a fundamental defect, or rather a series of defects, indeed a defective machinery is at the root of

---

42. Joint statement issued by the Bishops of the Mid-West Region, 11 August 2007.

contemporary economics and materialistic civilisation, which does not allow the human family to break free from such radically unjust situations.[43]

The challenge posed to us by Vatican II and by subsequent reflections is to recognise that the machinery is defective. We have arrived at a point to which the 'real world' planning has led us – and it is certainly no utopia. Surely it is time to ask fundamental questions! The logic of mere economic justice, of equivalence, which seeks to measure human exchanges only in terms of value and profit, is not enough. The market is not a mere machine, it is an instrument controlled by human beings according to their priorities and governed by human choices.

Pope Benedict argues that the purely profit-motivated approach to trade and commerce is not the only available one. There are other approaches already to be found:

> Alongside profit-oriented private enterprise and the various types of public enterprise, there must be room for commercial entities based on mutualist principles and pursuing social ends to take root and express themselves. It is from their reciprocal encounter in the marketplace that one may expect hybrid forms of commercial behaviour to emerge, and hence an attentiveness to ways of civilising the economy.[44]

For many years the Focolare movement has fostered what it calls 'the Economy of Communion'. It has set up small cities which operate on the basis of these principles. The first was in Loppiano near Florence. Launching a pilot project in the town of Araceli for the Economy of Communion in Brazil, the foundress of the movement, Chiara Lubich, 'challenged the 200,000 members

---

43. JOHN PAUL II, *Dives in Misericordia*, 11.
44. *Caritas in Veritate*, 38.

of the Focolare Movement in Brazil to establish businesses around Araceli to create jobs in the region. She proposed to all those who chose to become shareholders of these businesses to freely give one third of the profits for capital reinvestment. The remaining two thirds would be allocated to those in need and for the development of structures for the formation of people in the values of the "culture of giving".'[45]

One should also recall the Cooperative Movement in Ireland, which from the foundation of the first dairy cooperative in Dromcollogher, Co. Limerick in 1889, numbered eighty-seven units by 1900 in addition to forty-six independent agricultural societies.[46] It is not impossible to change a culture.

Such thinking is not confined to papal encyclicals. The philosopher Paul Ricoeur said that 'the logic of generosity clashes head on with the logic of equivalence which orders our everyday exchanges, our commerce and our penal law'. And he argued:

> Is not our task at the national level, and even more at the international level, to bring about the economy of the gift within a modern context? Is not our task to rectify by some positive interventions, the inequality which results precisely from our application to all our economic and commercial relations of the logic of equivalence?[47]

The Compendium of the Social Teaching of the Church was written to provide 'a concise but complete overview'[48] of the Church's reflection in the social encyclicals, in the Council documents and in the work of bishops and scholars. It identifies three great challenges facing humanity.

---

45. BEINER, H., 'Economy of Communion', http://www.evrel.ewf.uni-erlangen.de/pesc/R2001-EoC.html; accessed 6 March 2012.
46. http://www.ucd.ie/archives/html/exhibit1.htm.
47. RICOEUR, P., 'The Logic of Jesus, the Logic of God', in *Figuring the Sacred,* Mark Wallace (ed.), Minneapolis: Fortress Press 1995, p. 283.
48. *Compendium of Social Teaching of the Church,* presentation by Cardinal Martino.

The first is to *understand the truth about who we are as human beings*. The relationships between nature, technology and morality require 'personal and collective responsibility with regard to the attitudes to adopt concerning what human beings are, what they are able to accomplish and what they should be'. The second is the challenge of '*the understanding and management of pluralism and differences* at every level: in ways of thinking, moral choices, culture, religious affiliation, philosophy of human and social development'. The third is *globalisation*, and not just in terms of economics, 'since history has witnessed the opening of a new era that concerns humanity's destiny'.[49]

The renewal of the Church and society in Ireland will be well founded if it is based on serious reflection on the true, great hope which comes from knowing who we are in the light of God's love revealed in Christ, who has become one of us.

> He worked with human hands, he thought with a human mind. He acted with a human will and with a human heart he loved. Born of the Virgin Mary, he has truly been made one of us, like us in all things except sin.[50]

If we really grasped the truth that the whole of creation is a gift of God, that all is gift, it would change everything. The principle of gratuitousness is fundamental not only to social issues but to the whole of life:

> Because it is a gift received by everyone, charity in truth is a force that builds community, it brings all people together without imposing barriers or limits. The human community that we build by ourselves can never, purely by its own strength, be a fully fraternal community, nor can it overcome

---

49. *The Compendium of the Social Doctrine of the Church*, 16.
50. *Gaudium et Spes*, 22.

every division and become a truly universal community. The unity of the human race, a fraternal communion transcending every barrier, is called into being by the word of God-who-is-Love. In addressing this key question, we must make it clear, on the one hand, that the logic of gift does not exclude justice, nor does it merely sit alongside it as a second element added from without; on the other hand, economic, social and political development, if it is to be authentically human, needs to make room for the principle of gratuitousness as an expression of fraternity.[51]

---

51. *Caritas in Veritate*, 34.

CHAPTER FIVE

The Door of Faith
is Always Open

THE FIFTIETH ANNIVERSARY OF the opening of the Second
Vatican Council will be remembered in Rome by two events
with a common focus. The Synod of Bishops will meet during
October 2012 to discuss the theme, 'The New Evangelisation
for the Transmission of the Christian Faith', and a Year of
Faith will begin on 11 October 2012.

The first Year of Faith was announced by Pope Paul VI in
1967 soon after the closing of the Council, and it began in 1968.
He saw it as an occasion 'to reflect again on the Church's *raison
d'être*, to discover again her initial energy, to express again in
ordered teaching the content and meaning of the living Word of
revelation ...'[1]

On the thirtieth anniversary of the opening of the Second
Vatican Council, Pope John Paul signed a document promulgating
the *Catechism of the Catholic Church*. It was designed to contain
'the new and the old, because the faith is always the same yet the
source of ever new light'. It presented its material in the traditional
order: Creed, Liturgy, Christian Life and Prayer. At the same time
'the contents are often expressed in a new way in order to respond
to the questions of our age'.[2]

All of this implies that the most important questions addressed
by the Council, and the most crucial implications for its fruits fifty
years later, are about faith itself. It points to the need for constant

1. PAUL VI, Homily on 29 June 1968, Solemnity of SS Peter and Paul, the begining of
the Year of Faith (my translation).
2. JOHN PAUL II, *Fidei Depositum*, Apostolic Constitution on the publication of the
Catechism of the Catholic Church.

renewal of the way that we communicate the unchanging faith in a changing world. Pope John Paul's homily in Knock clearly stated that need:

> [T]he task of renewal in Christ is never finished. Every generation, with its own mentality and characteristics, is like a new continent to be won for Christ. The Church must constantly look for new ways that will enable her to understand more profoundly and to carry out with renewed vigour the mission received from her Founder.[3]

In all the challenges we face in the Christian life of Ireland, the most fundamental is to foster a deep and vibrant faith. The Year of Faith is intended to remind us that the door of faith is always open and that 'It is possible to cross that threshold when the word of God is proclaimed and the heart allows itself to be shaped and transformed by grace.'[4] Like the generations that preceded us, the world of today has its own particular ways of making it difficult for the heart to allow itself to be shaped and transformed by grace.

TEMPTATIONS IN THE DESERT

In announcing the Year of Faith, Pope Benedict said:

> Ever since the start of my ministry as Successor of Peter, I have spoken of the need to rediscover the journey of faith so as to shed ever clearer light on the joy and renewed enthusiasm of the encounter with Christ. During the homily at the Mass marking the inauguration of my pontificate I said: 'The Church as a whole and all her Pastors, like Christ, must set out to lead people out of the desert, towards the place of life,

---

3. JOHN PAUL II, Homily at Knock, 30 September 1979.
4. BENEDICT XVI, *Porta Fidei*, Apostolic Letter for the Year of Faith, 1.

towards friendship with the Son of God, towards the One who gives us life, and life in abundance.'[5]

The image of the desert has many echoes today. It was in the desert that Jesus prepared for his mission of proclaiming his Father's word. The temptations in the desert were about factors which would have fatally damaged the preaching of the Gospel. He was tempted to turn stones into bread – to settle for the satisfaction of the immediate need for food; he was tempted to leap down from the temple and be spectacularly saved by God and so win the amazed admiration of the people; he was tempted to use power to impose his message, ruling all the kingdoms of the earth. These were designed to distort and undermine his mission of bringing the Good News to the world.

It is not that satisfying one's hunger, being popular, or exercising power are wrong in themselves. It is not that they may not on occasion provide possibilities for communicating the Gospel. The temptation is to *live for* these things, to put them in the place that belongs to God. Yielding to that temptation would prevent us from opening our hearts to the infinite God by persuading us to settle for lesser, ultimately unsatisfying goals. They are temptations to settle for something less demanding than the Gospel, but something that can never satisfy the restlessness of the human heart.

In some cases, the most important goals of a person's life might be things that can be owned and used, but turning the stones into bread would never be enough. That cannot be the meaning of our lives. Our longings are unlimited and no amount of possessions can satisfy them. The meaning of life is not to be found in what we have, but in what we are. No matter how valuable our possessions, 'we can't take them with us'. Human beings do not live on bread alone but on every word that comes from the mouth of God (Mt 4:4).

---

5. Ibid.

Jesus taught the same lesson to the crowds who came looking for him. He told them that they were only following him because they had eaten their fill of the loaves. He told them not to work for the food that perishes. 'This is the work of God,' he said, 'that you believe in him whom he has sent' (Jn 6:29).

Many people live as though making an impression on other people, being admired or, more nonsensically, being a celebrity, is the purpose of their life. We all need to experience love and affection, but the meaning of our lives cannot be found in the good opinion of others. The Pharisee who gave thanks that he was not like other men judged himself by comparison with others and in the light of how they saw him – or how he thought they saw him. He could not have been more wrong. 'Other people' do not know us very well; nor do we know ourselves very well. And there are few things in life as fickle as public opinion.

> Fame is a fickle food
> Upon a shifting plate
> Whose table once a
> Guest but not
> The second time is set.
> Whose crumbs the crows inspect
> And with ironic caw
> Flap past it to the Farmer's Corn –
> Men eat of it and die.[6]

We are tempted to settle for making power and influence the goal of our lives. Many a dictator has learned that it is never possible to guarantee that even the strongest ruler will not be toppled. On a smaller scale, ambition and the desire to control the course of events can become obsessions which distort the lives of individuals and of society and which must ultimately fail.

---

6. DICKINSON, Emily, 'Fame is a Fickle Food'.

Our present economic collapse owes a great deal to an atmosphere which gave to greed, to the pursuit of celebrity and to the ambition for power of various kinds – economic, political, forms of manipulation and propaganda – a place which was ultimately destructive of all concerned.

An important contributory factor in that atmosphere was that our culture does not leave much space for asking the fundamental questions: 'What gives my life meaning?' 'What is the purpose of all the activities that absorb my time and attention?' 'Is there any overriding priority or is my life only a jumble of competing demands?'

Pope Paul VI wrote of the need to bring the Good News to human cultures. What matters, he said, is to do so 'not in a purely decorative way, as it were, by applying a thin veneer, but in a vital way, in depth and right to their very roots ... always taking the person as one's starting-point and always coming back to the relationships of people among themselves and with God'.[7]

THE PERSON AS STARTING POINT

Pope John Paul's first encyclical says that if we enter into ourselves in the light of the Incarnation and Redemption, we find our true selves. That leads to adoration of God and wonder at ourselves. He adds that the name for that deep amazement at human worth and dignity 'is the Gospel, that is to say, the Good News. It is also called Christianity.'[8] That is a statement worth reflecting on – *our amazement at ourselves in the light of Christ IS the Good News.*

The human person is a mystery. If we try to understand ourselves as though we were simply objects which could be measured and dissected, we miss the real truth. The complete description of the physical reality of 'the human hand' is very different from my experience of 'my hand'. One could list all

---

7. PAUL VI, *Evangelii Nuntiandi*, 20. The reference is to *Gaudium et Spes*, 53.
8. JOHN PAUL II, *Redemptor Hominis*, 10.

the chemical components of a human body; one could list the complete genome of an individual; one could trace every detail of a person's physiology, anatomy and biology. None of that knowledge, useful though it may be, can even begin to answer the questions that are fundamental to the person's understanding of him/herself: 'Who am I?' and 'What is the meaning of my life?'

We are full of longings – for truth, for beauty, for goodness. We long especially to love and to be loved. If, therefore, our starting point is reflection on the human person, we come back to our relationships with one another and with God.

Faith adds a new and entirely unexpected dimension to those longings. Throughout history, human beings have come to believe in the existence of a personal God. But they did not dream that our relationship with God could be a two-way relationship of love, still less that it could be initiated by a God who loves us first (1 Jn 4:19).

Nor could human beings imagine that all of those longings could ever be fulfilled for the whole human race. Already millions upon millions have died without ever glimpsing a perfect world. It is impossible to imagine a world in which the political, cultural, economic conditions would be to the complete satisfaction of everybody.

The Good News is that what has occurred is beyond human imagining. Nothing could entitle us to expect that God would approach the creatures he had made out of nothing and offer them his friendship and a sharing in his life.[9]

God's approach to us is made out of sheer love. The friendship he offers in his Son is 'the goal of human history, the focal point of the longings of history and of civilisation, the centre of the human race, the joy of every heart and the answer to all its yearnings'.[10] Faith is our acceptance of that approach of love.

---

9. See *Dei Verbum*, 2.
10. *Gaudium et Spes*, 45.

Even that acceptance of God's offer is beyond us; it requires the help and power of the Holy Spirit, which we constantly need in order to grow in understanding and acceptance of the gift.[11]

For anyone who believes in the faith of the Judaeo-Christian revelation, the human person is not just a being who seeks truth, who yearns for beauty, who longs for goodness, who hungers for love. The unlimited Source of all truth, beauty, love and goodness has spoken to us and invited us to share the life in which all our longings, and those of every human being of every time and place, can be fulfilled. That is the basis for the adoration of God and the wonder and amazement at ourselves which is the Good News.

FAITH AND THE LIFE OF SOCIETY
Faith does not provide political programmes or economic directives, but it gives an understanding of the meaning of social living which can both inspire and clarify our perspective. Insensitivity to the questions about the meaning of life, to which religious traditions have offered an answer, can deprive social living of an essential foundation:

> Truly the world is dark wherever men and women no longer acknowledge their bond with the Creator and thereby endanger their relation to other creatures and to creation itself. The present moment is sadly marked by a profound disquiet and the various crises – economic, political and social – are a dramatic expression of this.[12]

One of the great untruths of contemporary life, one that is taken as self-evident by many, is that religion is destined to die out as the world becomes more enlightened. A young Frenchman,

---

11. See *Dei Verbum*, 5.
12. BENEDICT XVI, to the Members of the Diplomatic Corps accredited to the Holy See, 9 January 2012.

Alexis de Tocqueville, visited the United States in 1830 and wrote a detailed account of the new democracy. One of the things that struck him was that the assumption that religion would decay was not at all verified:

> The philosophers of the eighteenth century explained the gradual decay of religious faith in a very simple manner. Religious zeal, said they, must necessarily fail, the more generally liberty is established and knowledge diffused. Unfortunately, facts are by no means in accordance with their theory. There are certain populations in Europe whose unbelief is only equalled by their debasement, whilst in America, one of the freest and most enlightened nations in the world, fulfils all the outward duties of religious fervour.[13]

In the last decade or so, several studies have shown that this is still the case. Religion has not died, 'it is a fundamental and primary source of community and altruism'.[14] The illusion that the culture of the West is at the cutting edge of human development leads to an arrogant ignoring of the growth of religion in many parts of the world.

The valuing and deepening of faith would contribute enormously to the renewal of civil society – a point that is not well appreciated by many of those who are charged with the well-being of society. The problem lies, as Chief Rabbi Jonathan Sacks put it, 'in a certain emptiness at the heart of our common life'. He goes on to point out the fallacy of thinking that it is possible to 'edit God out of the language and leave our social world unchanged':

---

13. DE TOCQUEVILLE, A., *Democracy in America*, tr. Henry Reeve, ch. XVII, pt. III, Kindle Edition loc 6298.
14. SACKS, J., 'The Limits of Secularism', in *Standpoint*, Jan/Feb 2012, p. 72.

Something has been lost in our consumer culture: that sense of a meaning beyond ourselves that was expressed in our great religious traditions.[15]

Faith and the awareness of the questions about a sense of meaning beyond ourselves are not questions that concern only religious people. Those questions are at the root of art and literature and music and culture:

> At the heart of every culture lies the attitude the human being takes to the greatest mystery: the mystery of God. Different cultures are basically different ways of facing the question of the meaning of personal existence. When this question is eliminated, the culture and moral life of nations are corrupted.[16]

A society which has no place for reflecting on the meaning of life is an empty society. The marginalising of faith, and of fundamental questions of meaning, leads to many of the weaknesses of twenty-first-century Ireland and of the western world generally. Our economic and political systems are not working, but the fundamental problem lies in the failure to ask the basic questions. How can a system serve human beings and human society if it is not founded on any sense of the meaning of human life and of human relationships and does not explicitly acknowledge the importance of these issues in the lives of its citizens?[17]

FAITH AND THE GOOD LIFE

Both in individual and in social living many non-believers are admirable in their commitment to justice and their generosity. It is in no sense to diminish that admiration to say that the Gospel can renew and enrich human life in every context.

15. SACKS, J., *The Persistence of Faith*, London: Continuum, 1991, p. 26, 27.
16. JOHN PAUL II, *Centesimus Annus*, 24.
17. See Chapter 4, especially p. 98.

When Pope John Paul set out to address the issue of morality in today's world, he began with the story of the rich young man in Matthew, Chapter 19. The young man asked 'what good must I do to have eternal life?' Jesus points to the commandments, but it is clear that there is a deeper issue:

> For the young man, the question is not so much about rules to be followed, but about the full meaning of life. This is in fact the aspiration at the heart of every human decision and action, the quiet searching and interior prompting which sets freedom in motion. This question is ultimately an appeal to the absolute Good which attracts us and beckons us; it is the echo of a call from God who is the origin and goal of man's life. Precisely in this perspective the Second Vatican Council called for a renewal of moral theology, so that its teaching would display the lofty vocation which the faithful have received in Christ, the only response fully capable of satisfying the desire of the human heart.[18]

For some this may seem strange. We often speak as though the foundation of Christian morality could be found in the Ten Commandments. The *Catechism of the Catholic Church* also begins with the incident of the rich young man. It goes on to say quite explicitly:

> The Commandments properly so-called *come in the second place*: they express the implications of belonging to God through the establishment of the covenant. *Moral existence is a response to the Lord's loving initiative*. It is the acknowledgement and homage given to God and a worship of thanksgiving. It is cooperation with the plan God pursues in history.[19]

---

18. JOHN PAUL II, *Veritatis Splendor*, 7.
19. *Catechism of the Catholic Church*, 2062 (my italics).

For the person of faith, the meaning of life is to respond to the invitation of the Creator. Choices are not just a question of maximising happiness, however that is to be measured, nor is it about instincts; it is about searching for the truth, which is ultimately searching for God. Conscience is a person's attempt to find the truth, which for a Catholic will be enlightened by the long history of sanctity and integrity, and by that history crystallised in the teaching of the Church.

Every moral decision, whatever one's faith or lack of it, presupposes some sense of what life is for and what would make life good. This is true of the choices made by society also. It too needs a vision; 'Without prophecy the people become demoralised' (Prov 29:18, NAB). Clearly in the modern world we do not have a consensus about our vision for society, and this is one of the concerns that led the Holy Father to call a Year of Faith:

> Whereas in the past it was possible to recognise a unitary cultural matrix, broadly accepted in its appeal to the content of the faith and the values inspired by it, today this no longer seems to be the case in large swathes of society, because of a profound crisis of faith that has affected many people.[20]

How can there be any coherent approach to questions like 'How should I behave? What criteria should guide my decisions?' without some answer to the questions 'Who am I? Who are we? What is the purpose of our lives?'

For instance, an understanding of the human being as a particularly complex and wonderful machine will favour an approach which tends to evaluate human behaviour in terms of what the 'machine' produces. It will seek ways of testing the 'quality' of those results in terms of the consequences they

---

20. SACKS, *The Persistence of Faith*, p. 2.

'produce' for those affected by them. It will ask whether the consequences of this choice will cause happiness or pain and seek to measure the extent of each.[21]

But such an approach would not do justice to what a human person is, to human relationships, to an adequate vision of human life, to the nature of human freedom. We are not just machines producing results; we are free beings in relationships with others and with our Creator.

Whenever we exercise our freedom, we do more than choose a particular line of action. Our choice says something about the kind of person we wish to be – honest or dishonest, just or unjust, loving or selfish; it says something about how we regard the other people who may be affected – as my equal or as a means to the end of advancing my plans; it says something about how I see the goal of my life. Faith offers a context for understanding these aspects of human freedom in a way which is worthy of the goal to which we are called by God's gift and promise made known in Jesus Christ:

> 'Come, follow me', is the new, specific form of the commandment of love of God. Both the commandments and Jesus' invitation to the rich young man stand at the service of a single and indivisible charity, which spontaneously tends towards that perfection whose measure is God alone: 'You, therefore, must be perfect, as your heavenly Father is perfect' (Mt 5:48). In the Gospel of Luke, Jesus makes even clearer the meaning of this perfection: 'Be merciful, even as your Father is merciful' (Lk 6:36).[22]

There are many people who do not share the Christian faith but who, nevertheless, are in search of a sense of 'something beyond'.

---

21. See *Veritatis Splendor*, 74.
22. Ibid., 18.

They find that sense in art and culture, in the beauty of nature, in a relationship of love which says, however inarticulately: 'You, you in particular, will never die.'[23] What is crucial is that moral living is seen in terms of something beyond myself:

> I must puncture the illusion, infinitely persistent it is true, that I am possessed of unquestionable privileges which make me the centre of my universe, while other people are mere obstructions to be removed or circumvented, or else those echoing amplifiers whose purpose is to foster my self-complacency.[24]

FAITH AND SOCIETY

Two attitudes sound quite similar but are at opposite ends of the spectrum. One says, 'Society should be tolerant of differing religious beliefs'; the other says, 'What any individual citizen believes is of no concern to anybody else and it is irrelevant to the workings of civil, political society.' The apparent similarity depends on thinking about tolerance as if it were the same as indifference. In that case tolerance might be summed up as, 'Believe what you like, it's of no interest to me.'

The tolerance of religious beliefs in this sense can be dated back to the Peace of Westphalia (1648). This sought to end the divisions of the Thirty Years War by ensuring that each state would follow its ruler's will in religious matters, that citizens, whether Catholic or Protestant, would be equal before the law, and that individuals who did not share their ruler's faith could practice their religion publicly at specified times, and in private at any time. The hope was that this would prevent the emergence of future wars between people of differing religious beliefs.

---

23. MARCEL, G., *Homo Viator*, 1962, p. 147.
24. Ibid., p. 19.

One of the flaws in the reasoning is simple. Tolerance cannot be built on lack of understanding. Divisions are not avoided by keeping differences out of sight or refusing to address them. Hatred and bigotry are the products of ignorance: ignorance first of all of one's own position and ignorance also of the position of others. The person who, deep down, doesn't know where he or she stands is the one who will dismiss other people's convictions out of hand without any attempt to see those convictions from the other's standpoint:

> In real life the people who are most bigoted are those who have no convictions at all … Bigotry is the resistance offered to definite ideas by the vague bulk of people whose ideas are indefinite to excess.[25]

Another flaw is even more crucial. It is not the case that there is no relationship between faith and public responsibility. There is more to any human being than his or her role as a citizen of the state. Being a citizen is not the whole of our lives; there are areas of our lives which are not part of the structure of the state. The state is not a religious teacher, but those who exercise political power need to become 'fully aware of the urgent need to change the spiritual attitudes which define each individual's relationship with self, with neighbour, with even the remotest human communities, and with nature itself'.[26]

The role of faith in society is not to produce political or economic blueprints, but to strengthen and sharpen the foundations which democratic state cannot create for itself. The Church has a twofold role in relation to the state and to society:

---

25. CHESTERTON, G. K., 'Heretics', in *Collected Works*, Vol. I, San Francisco: Ignatius Press, 1986, pp. 201–2.
26. JOHN PAUL II, *Sollicitudo Rei Socialis*, 38.

... she is called to contribute to *the purification of reason* and to the *reawakening of* those *moral forces* without which just structures are neither established nor prove effective in the long run.[27]

Faith can purify reason. To give one example, my attitude to somebody, at home or abroad, who is poor or starving may be sharpened and made more realistic by the realisation that the Lord will speak to me *in his or her name*, saying 'I was hungry, thirsty, sick or in prison' and you did, or did not, show practical concern for me.

Faith can reawaken the moral forces which society needs in order to function. As with the moral behaviour of the individual, 'the full meaning of life' is at the root of any adequate understanding of the questions that arise. Our understanding of the basic issues, 'who are we?' and 'what is the purpose of our lives?' does not come from the state.

Jonathan Sacks points out that the values and convictions that are deepest within us are those we learn in our families, in our neighbourhoods and in our faith communities. That is 'where we learn who we are, where we develop sentiments of belonging and of obligation; where our lives acquire substantive depth'.[28] No doubt as we get older we adapt and we develop, but to become completely separated from these roots is to feel in some way adrift from oneself.

Sacks concludes that in a pluralist society each of us needs two languages. We have in the first place the language of our convictions, our faith, our sense of who we are and our sense of belonging to the human family. We also need what he calls 'the language of common citizenship' in which we communicate in terms of the common good, in terms of what would best serve

---

27. BENEDICT XVI, *Deus Caritas Est*, 29 (my italics).
28. See SACKS, *The Persistence of Faith*, pp. 66, 67.

the flourishing of citizens as individuals and as a society. In this common language we talk about what holds us together in the context of different world views.

That common language would be empty and lacking in moral force if each citizen did not bring to it the enthusiasm, the principles and the commitment that come from his or her vision of what gives meaning to life.

Furthermore, if there is no appreciation of the language of faith and conviction, there will be a constant temptation to think that everything in human life must be dealt with in the common language of citizenship. The state will feel that everything – moral values, education, a sense of belonging and so on – must be its remit, since there is no other source of meaning.

There are questions that cannot adequately be addressed except in the context of the fundamental questions about who we are and what life is about. Frank Sheed pointed out that if education is about preparing people for life, it is extremely odd for the state to think itself qualified in that area. The government is not elected or qualified or authorised by the citizens to decide about the nature of the human person or the meaning of human life.[29] How then can it imagine that it can prepare *people* for *life*? The best it can do is to prepare cogs for the economy. Teachers are not simply agents of the state. They act primarily on behalf of parents or guardians and the community.

Similar issues arise when the state and the civil law begin to be seen as the sole arbiters of right and wrong. We have become familiar with the consequences. The moral compass of society quickly loses its bearings:

> The gradual transformation by which sin becomes immorality, immorality becomes deviance, deviance becomes choice, and

---

29. See SHEED, F., *Society and Sanity*, London: Sheed & Ward 1953, pp. 3, 4.

all choice becomes legitimate, is a profound redrawing of our moral boundaries.[30]

If we were to reach a point where the only moral guide was the civil law, and public opinion, our sense of human freedom would be enormously diminished. Moral responsibility would no longer be seen as a response to the unlimited love of God or in the context of any overall vision of the meaning of human life.

OUR RESTLESS HEARTS

The human heart can be finally satisfied only by God. That is why the question of faith is essential to an understanding of human life. Faith is not just words; it must touch the heart; it has to speak to the deep longings of the heart. Those who profess their faith in routine words and actions may be further from the truth of God's Kingdom than agnostics who are constantly engaged in an honest search.[31]

Nevertheless, words are important. Faith has been expressed and clarified down through the centuries in the tradition of the Church. Clarifications which enriched our understanding came from councils and synods, from saints and theologians in the new situations in which believers found themselves; distortions which would have emptied the faith of its truth had to be challenged; faith took root in new cultures both enriching them and drawing new insights from them. There were many occasions when the integrity of faith could have been damaged by following mistaken paths.

It was a great adventure. The history of the Church is, as Chesterton put it, full of traps of error and exaggeration that it would have been all too easy to have fallen into;

---

30. See SACKS, *The Persistence of Faith*, p. 50.
31. See BENEDICT XVI, Homily in Freiburg im Breisgau, 25 September 2011.

But to have avoided them all has been one whirling adventure; and in my vision the heavenly chariot flies thundering through the ages, the dull heresies sprawling and prostrate, the wild truth reeling but erect.[32]

The heart of faith is not the words in which it is formulated, but God who speaks. Faith is first of all our assent to God and the entrusting of ourselves to God. But words are necessary because faith is not just an individual relationship with God. We believe within the community of faith. We speak to one another about our faith in words which are true, but which 'always fall short of the mystery of God'.[33] We try to communicate something of the truth and joy of faith to others in our words and actions. It is necessary that the Church, the community of faith, should be able to recognise the traps of error and exaggeration that could lead to a misrepresentation of the truth about God.

The issue of faith is at the heart of the renewal of the Church that was called for by the Second Vatican Council. The world needs faith more than ever:

> Our heart is restless for God and remains so, even if every effort is made today, by means of most effective anaesthetizing methods, to deliver people from this unrest. But not only are we restless for God: God's heart is restless for us. God is waiting for us. He is looking for us. He knows no rest either, until he finds us. God's heart is restless, and that is why he set out on the path towards us – to Bethlehem, to Calvary, from Jerusalem to Galilee and on to the very ends of the earth. God is restless for us, he looks out for people willing to 'catch' his unrest, his passion for us, people who carry within them the searching of their own hearts and at the

---

32. CHESTERTON, 'Orthodoxy', 1986, p. 306.
33. See *Catechism of the Catholic Church*, 42.

same time open themselves to be touched by God's search for us.[34]

SHARE THE GOOD NEWS

Efforts towards renewal for the Church in Ireland are focused by the fiftieth anniversary of the Council, by the Year of Faith and by the growing awareness of how vital those efforts are. It will be a long, demanding and unfamiliar road. The National Directory for Catechesis in Ireland, *Share the Good News,* will be a valuable roadmap. It provides an analysis of our cultural situation, and a picture of what is needed if we are to have 'a reinvigorated approach to teaching the Faith and sharing the Gospel'.[35] It makes it clear that this is a task in which every member of the Church, young and old, lay, religious and ordained, sick and healthy, Irish-born or immigrant, has to be involved both as a teacher and as a learner.

Perhaps the most striking contribution is how practical it is. It lists the resources that will be required and the objectives that need to be set at different levels – parish, diocese, episcopal conference, schools, groups and organisations; it speaks of formation for work in parishes, for teaching, for chaplaincy; it addresses the importance of resources and of inclusivity – together with indicators by which progress can be measured in all of these areas.[36]

That is the inescapable task that renewal of faith involves. It would be a tragic loss if this were to remain simply words on a page, nor should any Catholic think of it as something that other people will do. Let us make no mistake, the challenge to pass on the torch, the light of faith, in Ireland is as urgent today as it has ever been; the danger that this may be the generation that lets the torch fall is not to be taken lightly:

---

34. BENEDICT XVI, Homily, Solemnity of the Epiphany, 6 January 2012.
35. Irish Episcopal Conference, *Share the Good News, National Directory for Catechesis in Ireland*, Dublin: Veritas, 2011.
36. Ibid., Section D, pp. 189–220.

The challenge is now to revitalise our Christian lives and find the new direction that our times and circumstances require … Unless, however, we are willing to act as one, we will not know the full power that the Christian community has to transform our lives and the lives of others in God's love.[37]

37. Ibid., p. 224.